The Handbook of Lunchtime Supervision

Second Edition

Shirley Rose

Routledge
Taylor & Francis Group

LONDON AND NEW YORK

First edition published by David Fulton, 2006, titled *A Handbook for Lunchtime Supervisors and their Managers*

This edition published 2010
by Routledge
2 Park Square, Milton Park, Abingdon, Oxon OX14 4RN

Simultaneously published in the USA and Canada
by Routledge
270 Madison Avenue, New York, NY 10016

Routledge is an imprint of the Taylor & Francis Group, an informa business

Typeset in Celeste by FiSH Books, Enfield
Printed and bound in Great Britain by MPG Books Group, UK

British Library Cataloguing in Publication Data
A catalogue record for this book is available from the British Library.

Library of Congress Cataloging-in-Publication Data

Rose, Shirley.
The handbook of lunchtime supervision / Shirley Rose. — 2nd ed.
    p. cm.
  Rev. ed. of: A handbook for lunchtime supervisors and their managers, 2006.
  Includes bibliographical references and index.
  1. School lunchrooms, cafeterias, etc.–Great Britain. 2. School children–Food–Great Britain. 3. Recesses–Great Britain. 4. Playgrounds–Great Britain–Safety measures I. Rose, Shirley. Handbook for lunchtime supervisors and their managers. II. Title.
  LB3479.G73R67 2010
  371.114'1–dc22
                                                         2009020724

ISBN10: 0-415-49226-2 (pbk)
ISBN10: 0-203-86537-5 (ebk)

ISBN13: 978-0-415-49226-3 (pbk)
ISBN13: 978-0-203-86537-8 (ebk)

Contents

For my parents for teaching me so much

About the author

For many years I have been training school staff, mainly lunchtime supervisors and teaching assistants. I became interested in the work of LTSs some years ago when my son's excellent childminder told me about her 'other job' as a senior lunchtime supervisor at a local primary school in which, at that time, she had received no training. As a qualified social worker and Childline counsellor with many years' experience, I have an evangelical commitment to the importance of valuing and communicating with children. I am also convinced that everyone working with children needs training and support. With the help of a local head teacher I piloted a training package for primary school LTSs which I have since refined and delivered to many schools.

When I originally started this work, support staff were rarely given a voice or offered training. Thankfully this is changing. The hundreds of lunchtime supervisors I have worked with (in and outside the playground) have taught me how challenging, stressful and exciting their role can be.

Shirley Rose
London
January 2009

Acknowledgements

Many professional colleagues, friends and family members have helped in the writing of this book. Without their support and feedback, I doubt it would have been possible. I would especially like to acknowledge the help provided over the years by Peter Gordon and for his brilliant insight from the manager's viewpoint; the good natured and efficient assistance and feedback from Yvonne Rose (not to mention her impressive knowledge of punctuation); and the unstinting support, input and encouragement of John Crowther. I thank Louis Crowther for occasionally getting off my computer and Simon Crowther for getting on it and becoming my IT expert.

I would also like to thank Jenny Bloom for her early years advice, and Anne Watkinson and Julia Dowsett for their expertise. Thanks to Jude Clements for her healthy schools input and to Dave Thomas and Belle Amooty for their sporty education. I am grateful to Helen Ford and Viv Levy for listening to my moans, and to the Friday morning coffee group for encouragement and caffeine.

I am particularly indebted to the hundreds of lunchtime supervisors who have moved, enthralled and inspired me with their experiences, and to the many head teachers and school managers with whom I have worked over the years.

Introduction

A brief history of lunchtime supervision

In 1906, Parliament was successfully persuaded that hungry children had trouble learning, and the Provision of School Meals Act came into force, permitting local authorities to provide school meals. By 1939, less than 50 per cent of local authorities were providing this service for which families paid 2d (1p) for a meal unless entitled to free lunches. For many years teachers were required as part of their duties to supervise children at lunchtime. In 1968, following a long struggle, teachers won the right to have their own lunchtime break, although many continued to supervise lunchtime on a voluntary basis in return for a free school meal. Lunchtime supervisors were employed by schools prior to 1968, although their numbers and importance increased dramatically over the next few decades. The workforce remodelling agreement of 2003 aimed to free up teachers' time by employing and developing a vastly increased number of support staff. Schools now have the option of flexibly using a range of support staff to supervise the lunchtime period.

Lunchtime supervision in schools remains a subject of increasing importance. The original *Handbook for Lunchtime Supervisors and their Managers* was published in March 2006 and explored a range of relevant topics. This revised edition includes the exploration of three further developments:

1   The *Every Child Matters* agenda impacts upon every aspect of school life, and the lunchtime supervisor plays a fundamental role in helping children achieve the five outcomes.

2   Lunchtime supervisors are on the front line in the healthy food initiatives developed in schools, directly contributing to children achieving healthier lifestyles.

3   Schools organise the supervision of lunchtime in a variety of ways and are increasingly using a range of support staff, including teaching assistants and play leaders, to supervise lunchtime. The issues outlined in this book are relevant to teaching assistants undertaking lunchtime duties, and practice specific to this group is explored in greater detail. All staff who supervise lunchtime will be referred to as Lunchtime supervisors (LTSs) from now on.

Lunchtime supervision

As LTSs you have an important part to play in the success of the school day. Anyone who works in school will know that if the lunchtime goes well, teaching staff and children benefit, and the afternoon is likely to run smoothly. When the lunchtime break goes wrong, picking up the pieces can be time-consuming, disruptive and stressful. The majority of LTSs are required to supervise children for approximately an hour and a quarter per day, to ensure that they have lunch and the opportunity to play and let off steam. They are also involved in many important aspects of children's school experience including their eating, playing, friendship groups, behaviour and safety.

Staff who feel valued at work are more likely to develop higher self-esteem and motivation. This has not always been the case for LTSs, and throughout this book ways to include and support you will be explored.

From a management perspective

Managers will be aware that the lunchtime break is now being given greater importance. Ofsted inspections include an assessment of the behaviour of the pupils during lunchtime, and the new wellbeing benchmarks are relevant to a range of lunchtime issues. Many schools accept that they must put in the resources to ensure this part of the day is successful. Until recently, relatively little has been written by the government about the role of the LTS. In September 2005, as part of the behaviour and attendance pilot, a primary national strategy professional development pack was produced entitled *Playtimes and Lunchtimes* (DfES 2005a). This examines the contribution that well managed playtimes and lunchtimes can make to children's social, emotional and behavioural development. It also puts playtimes and lunchtimes into the context of a whole school behaviour policy, promotes practical strategies and considers the needs of staff who supervise this part of the school day. Very often head teachers express genuine concern about the difficulties LTSs face. They voice the desire to have an empowered and skilled team of staff who use their initiative to manage behaviour constructively so that problems do not escalate or spill over into the classroom. To achieve this, many head teachers now recognise that LTSs need to be provided with training and support.

What is in this book?

This book explores all aspects of lunchtime supervision. It looks at whole school practices that can contribute to happy lunchtimes and lunchtime staff and examines the necessary support, training and skills that LTSs require to do their job well. It includes examples of excellent practice developed in a range of primary schools and provides case studies and exercises to highlight how difficulties and pitfalls can be overcome.

The book is divided into two parts. The first part is for LTSs, although it is relevant for managers too. It comprises 11 chapters, described below, plus a brief introduction to the *Every Child Matters* initiative, and one shorter appendix focusing on LTSs' future learning and career development.

The second part of the book is particularly relevant to those who line manage LTSs and for senior managers responsible for the lunchtime break. It provides notes and good practice guidelines on each of the chapters (notes on Chapters 4 and 5 have been amalgamated due to the overlap in subject matter).

Also included in each chapter are activities which LTSs can do alone or with other members of the staff team. Managers may wish to use these activities in training sessions or meetings to develop their team's knowledge and skills. LTSs will need to feel comfortable enough to explore issues honestly and openly.

Introduction to the *Every Child Matters* initiative

The *Every Child Matters* (*ECM*) initiative affects the philosophy and organisations of schools in all areas, including their relationship with: the staff, children, parents and the wider community. It was originally developed following the tragic death of Victoria Climbié, an eight-year-old child who was tortured and killed by her great aunt and her boyfriend. Following extensive enquiries and consultations, the government published *Every Child Matters: Next Steps*, and passed the Children Act 2004. This provided the legislation for developing services to protect, support and improve the life chances and wellbeing of all children and young people.

Every Child Matters: Change for Children was published in November 2004 and describes how agencies must work together to ensure that every child from birth to 19, whatever their background or circumstances, will have the support they need to:

- Be healthy
- Stay safe
- Enjoy and achieve
- Make a positive contribution
- Achieve economic wellbeing.

This document outlines how all organisations involved with supporting and providing services to children, including schools, social workers, hospitals, the police and voluntary groups, are expected to share information and work together to protect children and young people from harm, and to help them achieve the above outcomes.

Developments

In March 2005, the first Children's Commissioner for England was appointed to give children and young people a voice and, in particular, to advocate on behalf of the most vulnerable (www.11million.org.uk).

The creation of children's services

In response to the *ECM* agenda, the Children Act 2004 set out requirements for the creation of children's services to deliver the authorities' education and social services provision to children and young people.

The Children's Plan

In December 2007, the government launched a £1bn, ten-year strategy for education, welfare and play. It outlined national and local priorities in tackling issues that directly affect children and young people. Following a lenthy consultation about children's hopes and concerns, it set out its goals which include: the development of play spaces, free childcare for disadvantaged two-year-olds, review of adolescent mental health services, review of sex education, better contact between schools and parents, better support for parents and children during and after family breakdown and more help for children with special educational needs. (For further information visit www.dcsf.gov.uk/childrensplan/downloads.)

Schools and the *ECM* agenda

Schools set out to improve outcomes for children and young people in a number of ways. These include:

- Helping each pupil achieve the highest educational standards
- Dealing with bullying and discrimination and keeping children safe
- Becoming healthy schools and promoting healthy lifestyles through Personal, Social and Health Education lessons, drugs education, breakfast clubs and sporting activities
- Ensuring attendance, encouraging pupils to behave responsibly, giving them a strong voice in the life of the school and encouraging them to volunteer to help others
- Engaging and helping parents in actively supporting their children's learning and development.

In *Every Child Matters: Change for Children in Schools* (DfES 2004) the goverment outlines how improving outcomes also involves narrowing the gap between disadvantaged children and their peers, and that greater support must be made available to parents, carers and families. It advocates that schools continue to raise educational standards by:

- Encouraging [them] to offer a range of extended services that help pupils engage and achieve, and building stronger relationships with parents and the wider community; and
- Supporting closer working between universal services like schools and specialist services so that children with additional needs can be identified earlier and supported effectively.

Children's centres and extended schools

The creation of children's centres (for children under 5) and extended schools were a response to the government's *Children's Plan* and the *ECM* agenda. They aim to offer support to enable children and families to improve their outcomes and to reach their potential. Extended schools and children's centres work in partnership with the local authority and children's trusts as well as voluntary, community and private sectors to offer access to a range of activities and services. In 2008, more than half of English schools provided some extended services, and by 2010 the government's aim is that all schools will provide facilities outside of school hours.

Research by Ofsted documents how these provisions improve children's learning and wellbeing: *How Well are they Doing? The Impact of Children's Centres and Extended Schools* (Ofsted 2008).

The Ofsted Inspection

A school inspection is carried out under section 5 of the Education Act 2005. It is a process of evidence gathering in order to provide an assessment of how well a school is performing. Inspections are short and focused, and dialogue with senior managers in the school plays a central part. The school's self-evaluation provides the starting point for inspectors, and the views of pupils, parents and other stakeholders are taken into account...It must result in a written report indicating one of four grades: outstanding, good, satisfactory or inadequate.

(From the Ofsted official website (http://www.ofsted.gov.uk/)

Schools are usually inspected at regular three-yearly intervals. The Ofsted inspection team ensures that the school contributes effectively towards the five outcomes. The new Ofsted inspection framework to be introduced in September 2009 will incorporate the new wellbeing benchmarks. These will include pupils' perceptions of how the school helps them to feel safe, protects them from being bullied and promotes healthy lifestyle. The take-up of school meals and the rate of attendance will also be monitored. In preparation for the Ofsted inspection, schools are expected to do a self-evaluation, analysing the impact that strategies are having, particularly in relation to the five outcomes in *Every Child Matters*. (For further information visit http://publications.teachernet.gov.uk and search for 'Ofsted inspection framework'.)

The role of the lunchtime supervisor in supporting the *Every Child Matters* outcomes

LTSs can actively support the five *Every Child Matters* outcomes to help children to:

- Be healthy
- Stay safe
- Enjoy and achieve
- Make a positive contribution
- Achieve economic wellbeing.

Each will be explored in greater detail at the end of each chapter, with the exception of Chapters 1 and 9.

Further information

The Children's Plan: Building Brighter Futures for Children (DCSF 2007) (visit www.dcsf.gov.uk/childrensplan/downloads).

Every Child Matters website (www.everychildmatters.gov.uk/).

Every Child Matters: A Practical Guide for Teaching Assistants by Rita Cheminais (David Fulton Publishers 2008).

Every Child Matters: Change for Children in Schools (DfES 2004).

Every Child Matters: Next Steps (DfES 2004).

Ofsted official website (www.ofsted.gov.uk).

Ofsted inspection framework (visit www.teachernet.gov.uk and search for '11 Million – The children's commissioner for England' (www.11million.org.uk)).

CHAPTER 1

The role and responsibilities of the lunchtime supervisor

Introduction

The lunchtime supervisor's work may be challenging, but it is rarely boring. As well as ensuring that children have lunch, and the opportunity to play, skilled LTSs are helping, and often teaching, children to eat, play, socialise, co-exist and deal with conflict and friendships. In other words, they are encouraging children to become rounded and civilised human beings. LTSs are required to keep large numbers of children safe, to manage their behaviour and to listen and respond to their problems (which may at times be serious). They are required to encourage healthy eating, to initiate and sustain play, to tolerate severe weather conditions, to prevent and respond to accidents, to be aware of bullying and to be sensitive to cultural and social issues.

Who becomes an LTS?

The majority of schools employ mainly female LTSs specifically for the lunchtime period; however schools may chose to organise the supervision of lunchtime using a range of support staff. As part of their contracted duties, some TAs are required to supervise all or

part of lunchtime. LTSs may also work as learning support assistants, site managers, cleaners or administrators. Other responsibilities may include welfare tasks, after-school youth work, bus escort duty and breakfast club supervision. In this book, all support staff who supervise lunchtime will be referred to as LTSs.

What are your main responsibilities at lunchtime?

ACTIVITY 1

Your role

List the main tasks you are required to do:

1 To keep children safe in the playground

2

3

4

5

6

7

8

Get together with other team members and compile a team list.

Responsibilities will vary from school to school. Your tasks are likely to include:

- Supervising the children in the playground and dining room
- Encouraging healthy eating
- Managing children's behaviour
- Keeping children safe
- Setting up the lunch area and clearing the dining room at the end of lunch
- Supervising children while they are queuing and eating
- Listening to children
- Recognising and responding to bullying
- Responding to disputes and fights between children
- Recognising possible signs of child abuse
- Assisting isolated or distressed pupils
- Responding to illness, accidents and emergencies
- Administering basic first aid
- Encouraging children to play constructively by initiating, sustaining and, at times, joining in with games
- Being responsible for playground equipment
- Supervising wet play
- Liaising with teachers and informing them about good and bad behaviour.

Clarifying your responsibilities

To be effective at work, you will need to be clear about your role and responsibilities. New LTSs often describe 'being thrown in the deep end' and 'learning on the job'. To clarify your position you will need:

- A job description outlining your duties and responsibilities. If you do not have one, ask your line manager for assistance
- User-friendly summaries of school policies in relation to behaviour, health and safety, child protection, food, bullying, inclusion, confidentiality and physical contact. Meeting time may be required to help team members understand how these policies apply to them in practice
- An induction pack and induction training
- Regular discussions with your line manager to reinforce good practice and to clarify issues of responsibility, accountability and confidentiality (see Chapters 1 and 2).

Ask for a relevant job description if you have not already been given one.

The main responsibilities of the LTS

Keeping children safe

One of the your most important duties is to keep children safe at lunchtime by maintaining order in the dining room and playground. You are also required to keep children safe from abuse and bullying. All schools will have a range of relevant policies outlining your responsibilities in relation to health and safety, safeguarding children and bullying, which will be discussed in greater detail in Chapters 6, 8 and 11.

Caring for children

Many LTSs describe how they care for the children in the way they would like their own children to be cared for. It is not unusual for younger children to call you 'mum' in error, and in one school the LTSs were nicknamed 'the dinner mummies'. Although you are not solely in a parental role, nurturing and supporting children are important parts of your job. You are also likely to be the person who deals with children's injuries and accidents, as well as distress and ill health. It is not surprising that if you listen well and develop positive relationships with pupils you are likely to be told their problems and secrets. This will be explored further in later chapters.

Instructing children

As an LTS you have the potential to be an excellent instructor or educator. For example, for a range of social or cultural reasons, when children start school they may never have learned to use a knife and fork or to eat at a table. You can sensitively teach a child to 'do things differently'. You can also teach children to share, to take turns, to negotiate and to express their emotions appropriately. How often do you find yourself reminding children to deal with conflict without resorting to violence? You can't wave a magic wand and *make* children get on, but you can teach them how to talk about their differences, to explore options, and to agree on solutions. LTSs regularly teach children how to play safely, to respect each other's food, cultures and customs, to empathise and to generally get along together.

Accountability

To whom are you are accountable?

Every member of staff in a school is accountable to somebody. To do the job well you will need to know who decides on your role and responsibilities. This is usually the head teacher or a senior manager, although the school governors will also have a say. This person will be referred to as your 'line manager' from now on. If you also work within other capacities in school you may have more than one line manager.

> ### CASE STUDY 1
>
> In one school the senior LTS, who only worked at lunchtime, supervised a team that comprised TAs and non-TAs. During meetings, issues of accountability were clarified to ensure that the TAs knew when to discuss concerns with her and when to discuss issues with their 'other' line manager, the SENCO. Team members were comfortable with the senior LTS's position of authority due to her high level of competence.

The role of the senior lunchtime supervisor

Many teams will opt to employ a senior LTS to manage and support the team, prepare and implement rotas, deal with the most challenging of children's behaviour and liaise with teaching staff. This role may be undertaken by a TA or a higher level TA (HLTA). On other occasions a senior LTS who only works at lunchtime may manage a team which includes TAs.

ACTIVITY 2

Accountability

When undertaking lunchtime supervision:

1 In what sort of situations do you feel the need to consult with a more senior colleague?
2 Who is your line manager?
3 Who determines your duties and work patterns?
4 To whom do you go when you have a personal problem that affects work?
5 Who do you ask when you are unsure of something?
6 Who do you go to when you are worried about a child who appears to be distressed?
7 To whom do you report a child's unacceptable behaviour?
8 If a child is not eating on a regular basis, who would you tell?
9 With whom do you share ideas for changing or improving work practice?

Each school will organise things differently. It may be that you are expected to talk to the Senior LTS, or you may be required to go straight to the class teacher or the head teacher. What matters is that you are clear and happy about the school's expectations.

ACTIVITY 3

Dilemmas

When working with teachers and other members of staff there are likely to be areas where the lines of responsibility are unclear. Lack of clarity can result in frustration and bad feeling.

Discuss these real life dilemmas in your team and decide who is responsible in each of the following situations:

1 Children had been told to remain in the dining room at lunchtime 'on detention' for bad behaviour that occurred in a morning lesson. Who is responsible for supervising the children?

2   It is a cold winter day and some children come into the playground without their coats. Who is responsible for ensuring that they wear their coats?

3   Your own son had started as a pupil in Reception and wants to be with you throughout the lunchtime?

4   Who decides about the use of playground equipment and whether children can use the grassy area of the playground?

5   A child is sick in the toilets. Who is responsible for cleaning it up?

6   A teacher fails to collect her class from the playground at the end of lunchtime. It is time for you to go home. Who should supervise the children?

7   A parent insists on waiting outside the playground at lunchtime and passing sweets to her children through the fence. Who is responsible for challenging her?

There may be other dilemmas that your team is struggling with. If so what are they? Discuss your concerns with your line manager.

Discussion points from the above activity:

Dilemma 1

If you are supervising the dining room then you are responsible for all children's wellbeing. LTSs and teaching staff should discuss the practicalities of supervising children who have been placed in detention.

Dilemma 2

It is your responsibility to ensure children are wearing their coats. The class teacher may also share this with you.

Dilemma 3

LTSs whose own children attend the same school often have an agreement with team colleagues that they deal with their child/children whenever possible. This avoids accusations of favouritism or concerns that the LTS is too busy caring for his/her own child to do their job properly. It is also better for the child.

Dilemma 4

A decision about the use of equipment and the use of the grassy area in the playground is ultimately a senior management decision. Ideally, you will be able to have your say.

Dilemma 5

Responsibility for cleaning up vomit or other accidents will vary between schools. Many LTSs have this as part of their duties, although some do not.

Dilemma 6

You are responsible for the children's safety until they are in the care of another responsible adult. You will have to stay with the children until another member of staff relieves you. The teacher's lateness will need to be tackled by a senior manager.

Dilemma 7

You may choose to politely challenge the parent. If you feel unsafe or concerned, request back-up from a senior manager.

Do you feel valued?

In your role as an LTS, it is crucial that you are valued and respected by members of the school community, including the teaching staff and the children. Schools will vary in the treatment of support staff and the systems they may have to raise your status. You also have an important part to play in gaining the respect of others by being open and professional and by communicating your needs assertively. If you are unhappy with the way you are being treated, try to find a positive way to express your concerns and say what you think could improve the situation. Good practice in this area will be described throughout this book (also see Notes for managers, pages 129–30).

TAs who undertake lunchtime duty often describe the advantages of continuity gained from working throughout the whole school day. As well as familiarity with the children, they tend to have greater knowledge of school procedures and regular contact with teaching staff. LTSs who do not have these advantages can at times feel excluded. TAs will regularly use the staffroom and, owing to the nature of their classroom work, will hopefully have good working relationships with teachers. LTSs who do not work in the classroom can often be unknown to teaching staff and have little direct communication with them. Having TAs in the LTS team can break down this barrier. TAs can encourage the LTSs into the staffroom and make them feel more a part of the whole school team. They can facilitate more of a two-way system of communication with teachers about children of concern. TAs can also share their knowledge of children's interests with LTSs and so they can work together to provide different stimulating activities.

Teaching assistants who supervise lunchtime often say that the day can be tiring, particularly if they do not get adequate time for lunch. They can also feel pressured by teaching staff that see lunchtime as less important than lesson time.

CASE STUDY 2

TAs who undertook lunchtime supervision were in conflict with the class teachers when they felt pressured to return to class without a proper break. A new head teacher tackled this by gradually changing the school ethos. She strongly believed that well resourced lunchtimes enabled better afternoon learning and ensured that all TAs could leave class promptly and have a proper break before resuming class duties. The team described how lunchtime duty was given equal priority with classroom work, and that teaching staff were encouraged to be as flexible as possible.

Confidentiality

Everybody who works in school needs to be aware of the importance of confidentiality. This means sharing certain information only with appropriate people. In schools, confidentiality can be complex. Every situation is different, and your action or inaction may have serious consequences. As part of a school staff team you are likely to be trusted with confidential information about the children you work with on a 'need to know' basis. This means that decisions are made, usually by a member of the senior management team, concerning who needs to know specific pieces of sensitive information about individual children and their families. All school employees have a professional responsibility to avoid sharing confidential information with anyone outside school unless they have been authorised to do so, and to avoid gossiping.

LTSs have the potential to form very close relationships with children, who may trust you with their personal problems. It is not unusual for young children to tell LTSs their concerns, including intimate details about their family life. You may also notice changes in children's behaviour or marks on their bodies. If you have any concerns about a child's wellbeing, it is your responsibility to pass this information on to an appropriate person. This will be discussed in detail in Chapter 11. TAs who undertake lunchtime duty are likely to have close relationships with, and know a great deal about, many of the children. You may know about friendship issues, who is being bullied and possibly who is experiencing family problems or abuse. This has obvious advantages, but can also create a number of dilemmas. You will need to share confidential information with other LTSs on a need to know basis.

LTSs often live near the school and have strong community links. You may have worked at the school for many years, or be a parent of children at your workplace. This can have advantages and disadvantages. LTSs talk of the pleasure of being greeted in the street or supermarket by friendly children and parents. On other occasions they describe the pressures of being quizzed or confronted by angry parents when they are off duty. In such situations it is important to control your personal feelings and to respond calmly and professionally. Avoid entering into arguments with the parents as this usually makes matters worse. Explain firmly that you are not currently at work, and if they would like to discuss things further they should arrange to see the class teacher or head teacher.

ACTIVITY 3

Confidentiality questionnaire

Discuss these situations in groups or pairs and decide what you would say or do:

1   You are at the local supermarket on Saturday and a parent from school tells you she is worried that her daughter's class teacher is picking on her.

2   You are in the playground after school collecting your own child when another mum asks you if her child is eating her dinner.

3   You are in the playground after school when a dad asks you why his son is behaving like a sissy and playing girls' games at lunchtime.

4   An LTS who knows that you have greater knowledge of a child's family problems than she does (from your work as a TA) asks you if this child has a social worker.

5   A parent threatens you verbally in the street and accuses you of hurting her child when you stopped a playground fight.

Giving information to parents

LTSs are frequently asked questions by parents about their children's behaviour or food intake. Some schools are happy for you to answer simple queries as long as the situation appears to be 'straightforward'; others clearly expect you to direct the parent to the class teacher or head teacher. Talk to your line manager about your school's expectations in relation to Activity 3.

Conclusion

Being clear about your school's expectations will help you to behave in a professional and confident manner. This in turn is likely to lead to greater job satisfaction and respect from others.

Communication systems within the school

Introduction

In this chapter we will consider systems of communication within the school. There will be a number of practical activities to help you develop your thinking and skills.

If you work at lunchtime only, in the light of your short working hours, very specific tailor-made systems of communication need to be created to ensure that you are well briefed and that you pass on information to others appropriately.

Information about the school

How informed do you feel about what is happening at school, and how do you find out about rule changes or events? In the worst scenario, do you learn about these changes from the children? How often are you introduced to new members of office or teaching staff or told when people are leaving? Many schools have developed excellent systems of communication to avoid such difficulties.

CASE STUDY 1

A team of LTSs complained bitterly when they were not told about the staff Christmas lunch, believing that, as they were not informed, they were not invited. Their line manager was extremely apologetic and assured them this had been the result of stressed staff and inadequate communication systems rather than deliberate exclusion.

CASE STUDY 2

A group of LTSs were exasperated when they were the only ones who came to school on an October Friday *not* wearing jeans. The whole school had decided to participate in a special fundraising *Jeans for Gene's day* without their knowledge.

CASE STUDY 3

The TAs, who also covered lunchtime, received the newsletter and attended staff briefings every morning. They used the staffroom and participated in INSET training on a regular basis. The LTSs who did work in the classroom rarely received these communications and tended to find things out in a random way. The TAs in the team often assumed their colleagues knew things, and did not have time to pass on relevant information. Following whole team training, systems were introduced to improve this discrepancy.

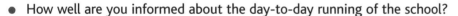

ACTIVITY 1

Discuss within your team:

- How well are you informed about the day-to-day running of the school?
- What systems are in place to inform you about important events?

Information about children

To work effectively with children you will need to be provided with an appropriate level of information about their health, diet, family circumstances and special educational needs. As described in the previous chapter, this information may be confidential and so shared only on a 'need to know' basis.

CASE STUDY 4

In a training session, one LTS described how she couldn't understand why a year 3 girl kept ignoring her instructions, until she was informed by another child that the girl was deaf. What systems could be in place to ensure such information is shared appropriately?

Information to be shared about children may include:

- A list of a child's special medical needs, displayed in a confidential place
- An up-to-date list of special dietary requirements, placed in an appropriately accessible, confidential place
- Sufficient details about a child's special educational needs. This may be discussed in meetings or communicated in writing
- Information about children who are bullying or are being bullied
- Strategies for managing children with particularly challenging behaviour
- Particular circumstances that may be affecting children including family problems (short term and long term).

ACTIVITY 2

Discuss the questions below:

- How well informed do you feel about the children you work with?
- What further information would help you to do your job better?
- What arrangements could be made to aid communication?

Communication systems

Effective communication systems include:

- Regular meetings with a range of relevant people
- Whole school training
- Sufficient and relevant written communication including internet-based systems for sharing information
- Structured verbal communication
- Handover systems before and after lunchtime
- Feedback following 'serious incidents'.

Meetings

Meetings can be time-consuming and difficult to organise during your limited working hours. Your school may have opted for a system where the senior LTS and the head teacher or line manager meet on a regular basis to share information which is then passed on to you. Many LTS teams also meet with their line manager to share information, to review practice, to feedback on difficulties and successes and to discuss training needs and school developments.

Many schools fix meetings on a regular termly or half-termly basis for approximately 30 minutes, usually immediately before or after lunchtime duties. LTSs should be paid overtime to attend.

Prior to a meeting, hopefully you will be encouraged to contribute to the agenda and to raise issues of importance. Not everyone speaks in meetings, and sometimes LTSs feel it is not their place to express an opinion. You are an important member of the school community who has a right to have your say. Once your team and your line manager have agreed to meet, it may help if you share the responsibility for making the meetings happen. To ensure that decisions made in meetings are acted upon, you should keep notes and refer to these at your next meeting.

Teaching assistants who undertake lunchtime duty can also feel pressured by teaching staff to remain in class. This can make attending meetings difficult.

CASE STUDY 6

In one school, TAs were unable to attend meetings with other lunchtime staff as their classroom duties were seen as a priority. This led to frustration within the team, as there was no forum to discuss differences or to develop good practice.

If you are not having meetings, or you are not being paid to meet, raise this with your line manager. If decisions made at your meetings are not put into action, find an appropriate way to voice your concerns.

advice

The role of the line manager as a 'go between'

As demonstrated by the case study below, following the meeting your line manager will be able to liaise between you and other staff groups to pass on concerns, feedback or requests.

CASE STUDY 7

In a meeting with their line manager (the deputy head teacher), a group of LTSs expressed frustration that teachers were allowing children to come into the school building for lunchtime clubs without informing them. Also, LTSs were not being told which children required an early lunch. The line manager agreed to remind teachers to give LTSs the appropriate lists of names and reinforce the rules in relation to children coming into the school building at lunchtime (a card system). At future LTS meetings progress on these areas was monitored.

The meeting as a forum for sorting out team relationships

You may be working in a team, often under pressure, with limited support. This can result in low morale and conflict between staff members. Anyone who has worked in 'unhappy teams' will know how unpleasant it can be. The case study below shows an example of a team who needed help to move on.

CASE STUDY 8

During a training session a senior LTS voiced her concerns about a breakdown in team relationships resulting from a bitter disagreement between two team members. This was clearly interfering with their effectiveness as a number of LTSs were refusing to talk to each other or even to sit around the same table. Following unsuccessful attempts to resolve their differences, the team agreed that they would seek help from their line manager. A meeting was called to air differences and to agree on acceptable behaviour whilst at work.

> **CASE STUDY 9**
>
> At monthly lunchtime meetings, the TAs tended to express themselves more assertively. However, they felt frustrated that their colleagues left them to do all the talking, particularly about controversial issues. At the same time, the LTSs were feeling dominated by their TA colleagues. They were eventually able to discuss this situation. Clearly a hierarchy had been established without people realising.

If you are struggling with similar issues, find a trusted person to assist you and your team. Although such discussions can be difficult, they can also be extremely productive.

Meetings without the line manager

You might meet on occasions as a team without your line manager to review your work and to support each other. This will need to be agreed by senior management subject to money being available to pay overtime.

Meetings with other staff members

In some schools, LTSs meet with the class teacher in the first few months of the school year for a short period to share relevant information about the children in the class.

If you have special responsibility for the nursery and reception pupils (early years), the infant pupils (key stage 1) or the junior pupils (key stage 2), meetings may be specially arranged for these groups. You may also benefit from occasional meetings with the Special Educational Needs Co-ordinator (SENCO) to discuss how best to respond to children with special needs or behavioural problems.

The use of INSET training to develop consistent practice

Many schools use INSET days to offer staff the opportunity for joint training and consultation. Sessions may focus on school rules, routines and policies, and encourage staff groups to discuss their expectations to ensure consistent practice. Sometimes LTSs describe feeling unwelcome or intimidated by the idea of attending whole staff training. However, if the subject is relevant, you are likely to be able to offer some valuable ideas.

> **CASE STUDY 10**
>
> A group of LTSs expressed their frustration at being required to sort out equipment cupboards on INSET days, whilst teaching staff discussed more important issues. They voiced their concerns and it was agreed that they would be invited to relevant sessions. The next INSET day focused on playground behaviour.

> **CASE STUDY 11**
>
> The children in one school often chose to relate to the TAs who worked at lunchtime as they felt more confident about the response they would be given. This created resentment within the team and senior managers offered INSET training to the whole LTS team to help them to build more positive relationships with pupils. The TAs also shared strategies that they had learned from working with the children in other settings.

ACTIVITY 3

Lunchtime staff meetings

Discuss the following questions briefly:

1   How often does your team meet with the line manager?
2   If meetings are *not* happening, would you like this to change?
3   Who decides on dates and times of meetings?
4   Do meetings take place at the agreed date or time? If not, do you request them?
5   Is there an agenda and if so do you contribute to it?
6   Do you meet *without* your line manager to review your work practices? If not, would this be helpful?
7   Do you ever meet with other members of staff, for example the SENCO, to discuss children with special needs? If not would this be helpful?
8   Do you attend whole staff INSET training when relevant?

Written communication including computer-based systems

Necessary written communication includes:

● Induction information
● The school newsletter for *all* LTSs – not just those who work in other capacities or who are parents of children at the school
● Lists of dates of school terms, INSET days and other events
● Minutes from relevant meetings including those that you were unable to attend
● A message or briefing book where information is written by teaching staff about children's needs or difficulties
● Lists of children's allergies, medical and dietary needs
● Information/staff briefings written on a daily basis
● Lists of children attending lunchtime clubs, outings etc.
● The detention book
● Forms, slips or books that enable information to be passed between LTS and other staff
● Copies of guidelines outlining relevant policy and procedures.

Communication systems require the co-operation of all staff members. Written information needs to be: accessible, relevant, up to date and, when necessary, confidential.

Computer-based systems

The Department for Children, Schools and Families (DCSF) has set the goal for all schools by 2010 to establish internet-based learning, teaching and communication systems known as the Managed Learning Environment (MLE) (visit www.teachernet.gov.uk for more information). This enables parents children and all staff, with the use of a password, to access and share relevant information. Many subjects listed above could be accessible on the computer system and training and support can help LTSs to feel confident to access it. You will also need time to check information on a daily basis.

Examples of good practice

In one school the head teacher was frustrated that the LTSs were not reading the message book in the staffroom on a daily basis. Following discussion it became clear that not all LTSs knew where the book was kept as they rarely used the staffroom. The book was moved to the general office.

In another school not all LTSs were receiving the weekly newsletter. It was agreed that a member of the office would photocopy it and leave it in the senior LTS's tray every Friday. The senior LTS would take responsibility for distributing it and feeding back if the system broke down.

Where is the information to be found?

Many schools view the staffroom as the centre of communication, where books or a whiteboard are placed to record and display ongoing information. If you do not use the staffroom, the school will need to develop clear alternative systems to ensure that you receive this information. The senior LTS or a team representative may take responsibility for reading the board, book or website and passing on relevant information to team members.

 If you are not using the staffroom, consider why this is.

Systems for sharing written information

There are many ways in which staff can share written communications and you will need to agree upon effective systems that suit you and your school. LTSs may have their own trays, pigeon-holes or interactive space on the school website to aid communication. Others have a noticeboard in a confidential place where relevant information can be displayed.

Your school will also need to ensure that information is updated regularly and distributed on time, as demonstrated by the example below.

The relationships within the LTS team became stressed when some members decided that others were failing to pull their weight. LTSs were extremely frustrated when they were required to cover for absent colleagues at short notice. The problem was two-fold: some LTSs were leaving it until the last minute to phone in sick, and office staff were not reliably notifying the senior LTS about the telephone calls in time for her to plan cover. Following a constructive planning session, feelings were aired and systems were clarified. It was agreed that anyone who was unable to attend work would phone and leave a message with the office staff by 9.00 a.m. The senior LTS would be notified of any phone calls in writing by the office staff when she arrived for duty.

ACTIVITY 4

Discuss the following questions:

- Do you have a pigeon-hole, trays or websites for written communications?
- What types of written communication do you receive?
- Would an LTS noticeboard be helpful?
- Who ensures that information about children is updated regularly?
- Who ensures written communication gets to the correct place?
- How could these systems be improved?

The handover of information

Schools benefit from structured handover of information before and after the lunchtime break. This ensures that LTSs are provided with relevant information about the children, and that teaching staff know what happened during lunchtime. This also helps children to see the lunchtime break as a consistent part of the school day, and to know that the appropriate people will know about their behaviour, both good and bad.

Handover arrangements will vary and can be by word of mouth or in writing. As always, the amount of information to be shared is important as too much or too little can be problematic. You may be required to attend a five-minute handover meeting with the senior LTS or a member of teaching staff prior to the commencement of duty. Alternatively, if you collect the same class of children each day, the class teacher will be able to share relevant information.

Feedback is often given to teachers by LTSs when they collect their classes from the playground at the end of lunchtime. Sometimes teaching staff complain that too much or too little information is being given. Before and after lunchtime, written information may be exchanged in a book or on special forms. It is crucial that all involved are conscientious about recording and reading the relevant information.

Feedback following serious incidents

LTSs often worry that feedback given to teaching staff is not always taken seriously or dealt with 'properly'. You are likely to feel better if you are informed about action taken by teaching staff or senior managers.

If you are not being given feedback, request it from the appropriate person.

Debrief within the LTS team following the duty

Many LTS teams describe the benefit of having time after lunch to talk about the session and to offer each other feedback and support. Some schools pay staff for an extra five minutes per day. Some educational authorities provide their LTSs with a free daily lunch so that they can eat, talk and unwind.

Every Child Matters – communication systems at lunchtime

The table which follows looks at information that LTSs need to contribute to the life chances and wellbeing of children at school. It focuses on the five *Every Child Matters* outcomes.

ECM outcomes	Schools will need to develop communication systems to ensure that LTSs have access to:
Be healthy	Health and safety, food, policy and procedures
	Information about children's medical issues, dietary needs, allergies and special educational needs
	First aid information
	Rotas for playground activities
	Healthy menus and other information about food-related issues
	Information about social and emotional development initiatives relevant to lunchtime
	Information about children's social and emotional issues and friendship problems on a need to know basis
Stay safe	Behaviour policy and lunchtime rules
	Behaviour plans and strategies to manage individual children
	Policies, procedures and information on safeguarding children
	Information about individual children who are being abused on a 'need to know' basis
	Health and safety policy and procedures
	First aid rotas and information
	Accident and emergency procedures
	Information about children's illnesses, disabilities, medical and dietary needs
	Anti-bullying policy, procedures and initiatives
	Information about children who are being bullied on a need to know basis
Enjoy and achieve	Rotas for playground activities/sports
	Play equipment and wet play activities
	Menus and healthy eating options
	Reward systems
	SEAL and other information to encourage pupils' social and emotional development
Make a positive contribution	Rotas for buddies and other playground initiatives
	School council information if relevant
	Involvement of children in a range of initiatives in the playground or in the dining room
	Questionnaires/systems for consulting pupils
	Strategies for conflict resolution to be used with pupils
Achieve economic wellbeing	Initiatives and strategies to develop pupils' organisational and leadership skills, buddy schemes and mentors

Conclusion

Schools are extremely busy and complex places and special attention will need to be given to developing systems of communication. For the lunchtime to be a positive part of the day and for LTSs to feel included, a large amount of relevant information must be shared. In this chapter a range of systems and practices have been explored and examples of good practice have been highlighted.

Further information

Virtual learning environments – visit:

http://www.teachernet.gov.uk/teachers/issue52/secondary/features/AseasyasVLE

http://publications.teachernet.gov.uk/default.aspx?PageFunction=productdetails&PageMode=
publications&ProductId=15003&

Building positive relationships with children

Introduction

As lunchtime supervisors you are often in an excellent position to build relationships with children. Unlike teaching staff, you have opportunities to play with and talk to children during less structured parts of the day. If you succeed in developing positive relationships with the children, you are more likely to mange their behaviour constructively and to become an important person in their school life. TAs who undertake lunchtime duty are likely to already have close relationships with, and know a great deal about, many of the children. The lunchtime period, however, enables you to interact with a wider range of children in a very different setting.

In this chapter the necessary skills for building positive relationships will be explored, including: ways to gain children's trust, how to listen, how to be child-centred and how to

help children cope with their emotions. It will also discuss ways to find the correct balance between fun and firmness, how to become a positive role model and the factors that interfere with building positive relationships with children.

There will be a number of practical activities to develop your thinking and skills.

How do you build positive relationships with children?

ACTIVITY 1

List a number of ways you develop positive relationships with the children you work with.

1

2

3

4

5

6

These might include some of the following:

- Learning their names
- Being child-centred
- Offering praise and showing children that you have confidence in them
- Appearing and sounding positive
- Listening
- Responding sensitively to what you hear
- Being consistent, firm and fair
- Being a positive role model

These issues will be discussed below.

Learning names

Using a child's correct name is a way to reach out to them. Calling children 'sweetheart' or other such names is not quite so personal. Learning names takes time, depending on your memory and on the size of the school. In multicultural communities children may have less familiar names and remembering these with the correct pronunciation demonstrates your respect. LTSs who do not work as teaching assistants often know the names of children who misbehave. There are a range of games that you can play with the children to help you learn their names. These include being tested by the child on a daily basis until you get their name correct or playing guessing games with the help of clues.

Being child-centred

When doing Activity 1, you may have included examples of being child-centred. This involves understanding what is happening from the child's point of view. It is not always easy to be child-centred, especially when a child's behaviour makes you angry or frustrated.

ACTIVITY 2

Becoming child-centred

Think of a particular age group of children that you work with and try to answer the following questions:

- Can you remember being this age?
- Have you had or do you have children or family members of your own who have been this age?
- What do these children find interesting?
- What sort of ideas and communication can they understand?
- What do they find amusing?
- What worries them?
- What matters to them?
- How do these children get on with their classmates?
- How different are the boys and the girls?
- How do children of this age cope with children who are from other cultures?

Examples of child-centred behaviour

- Talking to children about what interests them
- Sharing *appropriate* information about yourself
- Seeking children's opinions
- Using humour carefully
- Playing and joining in with games
- Accepting children, 'warts and all'
- Showing children that you can understand and help them to cope with their feelings
- Using appropriate touch.

Talking to children about what interests them

When you get to know children you will learn about the games, food and music they enjoy, their favourite TV programmes or computer games, their friendship groups, family holidays and festivals, and probably many other personal details. As a child-centred LTS you will try to show interest in what matters to the children and encourage them to talk about their world. You will speak in a way that children can understand, whilst being sensitive to their family circumstances and culture.

Sharing appropriate *information about yourself*

Many LTSs choose to share information about themselves and their family. This can be a helpful way to engage children's interest and makes you real to them. LTSs may choose to tell children about times in their own life when they experienced difficulties at school. This is usually intended to help children to feel that their worries are understood. However, care should be taken to avoid unnecessarily burdening or worrying children. It would be unhelpful, for instance, to talk about a painful illness or death in your family as the child is likely to sense your distress. Similarly, think carefully before talking about your own personal beliefs.

CASE STUDY 1

Following the death of a child's grandparent, an LTS attempted to comfort her by saying 'Granny has gone to Heaven'. She later realised that this had been inappropriate, as the child's family may not share a belief in Heaven. In such situations, be guided by the child.

Seeking children's opinions

In May 2008 the DCSF produced guidance that promotes the participation of children and young people in decision-making in school, local authority and related settings – *Working Together: Listening to the Voices of Children and Young People* (DCSF 2008). You can also demonstrate your confidence in children's ability by requesting help with tasks and initiatives and seeking their opinions

Using humour carefully

When we use humour appropriately with children we are saying, 'I like you and I want to be playful'. It helps to lighten a situation, and laughter is well known for its psychological benefits. Obviously, we need to be sensitive about the type of humour and the words we use. Avoid sarcasm as it can be confusing and can also damage self-esteem. Children of various ages and experiences will react very differently. A comment that a six-year-old might find funny could be offensive or embarrassing to a ten-year-old. You will also need to know when to change tack and when to respond firmly.

Playing and joining in with games

Many of the most enthusiastic LTSs describe the pleasure of joining in and playing with children. This will be discussed in detail in Chapter 8.

Accepting children, 'warts and all'

Children can be funny, spontaneous and loving. They can also be selfish, unkind, cheat, and tell lies. This is normal behaviour but it can leave you feeling angry or appalled. The real task is to try to accept that children behave in negative ways often for a range of reasons. Your role, therefore, is to help children to deal with their emotions more positively.

LTSs describe feeling furious when children lie. You may have witnessed a child's involvement in a playground incident, only to be told minutes later by the offender, 'It wasn't me'. It may help if you can view this as an immature way of wriggling out of trouble. Telling lies is a normal stage of development, which children usually grow out of. For some it is a sign of a more serious emotional problem. When dealing with lies, feed back to the child that their behaviour is unacceptable without being too punitive, and encourage them to deal with the situation in a more mature and honest fashion.

Helping children to understand and cope with their feelings

Children often experience their emotions intensely. The adult's role is to help children to understand and to talk about their feelings rather than to act on them (often in the form of misbehaviour).

In the playground, children have to manage challenging situations, particularly when they are learning to get on with others. They will experience a range of emotions including anger, elation, excitement, frustration and distress. In such situations, rather than giving advice or telling children what to do, try to demonstrate understanding.

If a child is showing anger, you may find yourself tempted to say something like, 'Calm down and stop being so silly'. Alternatively, you could try putting into words the emotion that the child is experiencing. For example: 'I can see that you are angry, but shouting like that won't help to change your friend's mind'. Or, when a child is distressed by losing a game, rather than saying, 'Never mind, you will win next time', you could say, 'I know it can be upsetting to lose; most people feel disappointed when it happens'. This can have a surprisingly calming effect.

There are many other ways in which LTSs can help children to manage their feelings – see the case studies below.

CASE STUDY 2

During a training session a team of LTSs described how they made a special arrangement with a year 5 pupil who was finding it difficult to control his temper. Whenever he felt he was about to 'blow' he would find an LTS who would give him a few minutes of calming-down time.

CASE STUDY 3

A teaching assistant, who also undertook lunchtime duty, worked in class with a young boy with Asperger's Syndrome. She encouraged him to be independent during lunchtime but offered him reassurance when necessary. She also helped other LTSs to manage the child when he became distressed.

Another way to help children to understand the language of feelings is to describe how children's behaviour is affecting you. For example, you can say something like, 'When you turn your back on me, I feel really fed up'. This is an example of demonstrating to the children how *you* would like *them* to express themselves.

Using appropriate touch
Many LTSs describe how they touch children as a way of showing affection and to build relationships. This needs to be done carefully and will be discussed further in the Chapter 11.

Offering praise and showing children that you have confidence in them

Children crave attention, and so by commenting on and praising a piece of behaviour it is more likely to be repeated. Genuine positive attention builds self-esteem as well as improving behaviour. Descriptive praise involves commenting on the desired behaviour in some detail. Rather than saying 'good boy' when a child shares equipment, try saying something like, 'I am really pleased with the way you shared your game with Simon. It's made him much happier.' This sort of praise has much more meaning and impact.

With older children, in particular, you can show that you have confidence in their ability to sort out their own disputes and arguments. Rather than feeling that you have to solve every disagreement, it may be helpful to ask the involved children what *they* could do to sort out their difficulties.

Appearing and sounding positive

In the light of the stresses of your job you cannot always look friendly and relaxed. You do, though, want to give the message that you are caring and approachable. In every day we can sometimes be unaware of how we appear to others. We communicate a great deal by our body language, which includes how we look, use our face and our eyes, our hand movements, gestures and the way we hold our bodies.

> **CASE STUDY 4**
>
> In a training session one LTS described how she had a tendency to look grumpy or fierce even when she didn't mean to. She realised that she rarely smiled and often frowned when worried or when she couldn't understand what a child was telling her. This explained why the younger children, in particular, often appeared cautious and uncomfortable in her presence.

LTSs describe how there is often an element of acting required in their work. Although children are likely to know if you are being insincere, learning to communicate positively is an important skill to develop.

Your tone of voice and use of words

Your tone of voice matters. LTSs describe how they try to speak in a warm, open tone. It can also help to lower your pitch and to speak slowly and clearly. You will need to ensure that the children understand what you are saying and that you are using words that are appropriate to the child's age and understanding.

ACTIVITY 3

How do you appear and sound when communicating with children?

Do you often:

- Smile?
- Frown?
- Maintain friendly, interested eye contact?
- Glare?
- Nod your head in an encouraging way when listening?
- Use your hands when you are angry?
- Point your finger, clench your fists, stab the air or fold your arms in front of your body?
- Shout at the children?

Think about the way you sound when you are angry. Is your tone calm and firm, or do you become high-pitched. How quickly do you speak?

Ask a trusted colleague for some feedback about the above points. You may not agree with their feedback, but at least you have a chance to learn about yourself.

Listening

Listening to children is one of the most important ways to build positive relationships. Many adults have a tendency to ignore, contradict, or rush children when they are talking. We may also finish their sentences, or tell them what they are thinking or feeling. It may be difficult to give them the attention they deserve when different groups of children are demanding attention at the same time, or you are called away mid-discussion to deal with an accident or a fight. Effective LTSs make a considerable effort to find the time to listen when they feel there is an issue of importance.

ACTIVITY 4

Think of reasons why it is important to listen to children.

1

2

3

4

5

Your list might include some of the following:

- Listening helps to builds good relationships
- We all need to be listened to as it helps us to feel valued, respected and cared for
- Children's self-esteem will suffer if they are not listened to
- Listening helps us to understand 'what happened', especially if the participants disagree
- Listening helps children to feel we are being fair
- Children often have important things to say
- We may hear about serious problems including child abuse or bullying
- We want to encourage children to express themselves.

Active listening

Listening is a skilled activity which involves:

- Looking interested
- Hearing what is said
- Remembering what has been said
- Checking you understand what is being said
- Trying not to interrupt until the child has said what they need to say.

(Adapted from Burnham and Jones 2002)

Open and closed questions

When a child is telling you something, you aim to understand as fully as possible what they are trying to communicate. One way to do this is by asking an open question. This is a question that encourages the other person to describe in their own words what they think or feel. When asking open questions, you can use words like 'Tell me about', 'Why', 'How' and 'What'.

A closed question has a *yes, no* or one-word answer. Such questions 'close down' the discussion. When you ask a closed question you use words like, 'Is it because?' or, 'Do you want to...?'. There are times when closed questions are useful, for example when you will not have time to listen, or when you need children to do what they are being told immediately. Generally, when you are trying to understand something, it is helpful to ask open questions.

Example

If a child says, 'I hate school', and looks distressed, hopefully you will find the time to understand what is upsetting them by asking an open question. You might say:

Why do you hate school?

What do you hate about school?

What happened at school?

You will then need to listen carefully to the child's response and, if still unclear, ask another open question.

A closed response to the same statement, 'I hate school', would be:

Is it because your best friend is away?

Is it because the work is too hard?

Of course you like school. Aren't they the best days of your life?

In response, you are likely to get a 'yes' or 'no'. It is helpful to practise asking open questions.

ACTIVITY 5

These are all closed questions. Can you re-phrase them with open questions?

1 Was your test hard?
2 Is your teacher cross?
3 Do you hate PE?
4 Did she hit you?
5 Are you feeling upset?

No matter how well you try to understand what is happening to a child, they may not want to talk. We cannot make children tell us what is on their mind, but we can use a range of skills to encourage them. When a child is reluctant to communicate, you can try:

- Asking a different open question
- Changing the subject and returning to the problem later
- Asking the child if there is anyone else he/she would like to talk to. This is not a failure, as we all find different people easier to talk to at different times
- Suggesting that you are available at a later stage if the child wishes to talk to you.

You might need to report your concerns to the class teacher.

Listening to both sides of the story

Children sometimes complain that LTSs don't listen or do anything about their problems. It helps to be extremely clear with the children about how you intend to sort things out. For example, when children are in dispute, it is important that you are seen to be fair by listening carefully to both sides of the story. Ask each child (or group of children) to take turns to say what happened, and listen to each without interruption. Remove the audience of on-lookers, and allow the children involved in the incident to calm down if necessary. You can also summarise what you have heard and encourage the children to come to their own solutions whenever possible. If you need to take action, explain clearly to them what you are going to do and why you are doing it.

Responding sensitively to what you hear

As well as listening carefully you will also need to consider carefully how to respond to what you have been told or asked.

When children talk about difficult issues

Children can be extremely open about their lives and may choose to tell you personal and, at times, shocking information. There is no easy way to respond to a child's pain.

> **CASE STUDY 5**
>
> An LTS described her horror when an infant child told her 'out of the blue' that he was upset because his baby sister had died. She described how she became confused and speechless.

ACTIVITY 6

Think about how you would respond to a year 4 child who tells you:

1 Their mum is very ill
2 Their dad has left home
3 Their grandmother has just died
4 Their dad has a new girlfriend or boyfriend.

In such situations, LTSs often describe desperately wanting to make the child feel better. Some are tempted say, 'I'm sure mum will get better' or 'Dad will come back home soon'. It is unhelpful to falsely reassure children by promising happy endings. You also need to avoid asking too many questions.

The safest way to respond is to ask the child how he/she is feeling and to be sensitive to their response. The child has chosen to tell you their story for a reason, and if they do not want to talk about it, they'll let you know. If you are uncomfortable in this role, find someone else for the child to talk to and remember to inform the class teacher of issues of importance.

Answering children's questions

As a trusted adult you will be asked questions about a range of issues. When giving answers you will need to take into account the child's age and understanding as well as their possible reason for the query. Questions about death, sex, religion or illness may be difficult to answer, so before answering, consider your response carefully. You may decide to refer the child to another member of staff.

When children ask complex questions – for example, 'Why do mummies get so upset?' – rather than answering the question directly, attempt to understand what the child is trying to make sense of. If you feel uncomfortable about discussing such personal issues, you can encourage the child to talk to his or her teacher.

Confidentiality

When you build positive relationships with children and listen well, they are likely to confide in you. You are required to tell an appropriate member of staff if you are worried about incidents of child abuse, bullying, racism, family problems, emotional distress or any other issues of concern. Children will need to know that you will not gossip or share their confidences inappropriately.

This subject will also be discussed further in Chapters 6 and 11.

Being consistent, firm and fair

Lunchtime supervisors often describe the importance of having fun with children but also knowing when to draw the line and become firm. The need to be consistent and fair has already been discussed and these subjects will be revisited in Chapters 4 and 5.

Being a positive role model

It is easy to underestimate how important you can be to the children you work with. If you are good to them, you will be viewed as a positive adult to learn from and to model themselves on. Male LTSs have a valuable role, as they can show children an example of a caring man. Older LTSs can have a special 'grandparent' role and supervisors from ethnic minority groups will offer children the chance to relate to people from other cultures.

Children learn from what we do more than from what we say. LTSs often describe how children notice every detail, including their moods, their hair styles, their behaviour or their clothes. By observing, children are making sense of the way people behave and how adults can differ.

If you want children to be well behaved and respectful you will need to be well behaved towards them and show them respect. If you present as a genuine and honest person who is not afraid to apologise for mistakes, the children will learn how to conduct themselves in a similar way. This will provide them with a positive role model.

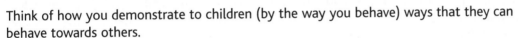

ACTIVITY 7

Being a positive role model brings with it a range of responsibilities.

Think of how you demonstrate to children (by the way you behave) ways that they can behave towards others.

1
2
3
4
5
6

Your answers might include:

- Being polite
- Being respectful in the way you talk to children
- Being fair and listening to both sides
- Being open and friendly
- Being encouraging and accepting
- Explaining why you want things done
- Talking about your own feelings when appropriate
- Being honest and saying when you don't know something
- Apologising when you make mistakes.

Factors that can interfere with building positive relationships with children

Communicating with children who do not speak English

There are various ways to develop relationships with children who do not speak English. These include the use of non-verbal communication like miming, smiling and appropriate touch. You can also play games and use songs and rhymes. Give instructions by offering practical examples in simple language. Using another LTS or child to act as an interpreter can be constructive, as long as they are willing to help. Children in this situation often learn to speak English at an impressive rate.

Children whom you struggle to relate to

No matter how hard you try, or how skilled you may be, there are likely to be children whom you find it difficult to relate to. This may be the result of a personality clash, or a range of difficulties experienced by you or the child. Ask yourself what, in particular, you find difficult about them or who they remind you of.

It might help to know that if you are feeling like this, there is a good chance that other adults are experiencing similar emotions. Try not to take such 'failures' personally. Relationships with children will have their ups and downs, and progress will often come in small steps.

What happens when relationships go wrong?

When you have worked really hard to build a relationship with a child, you may feel desperately disappointed when things go wrong. This is not unusual, as children, and indeed adults, will resort to old ways at times of pressure or crisis. Try not to take this too personally, and try to rebuild the relationship. Progress with troubled children comes in very small ways, and everyone will have off-days. Strategies to rebuild relationships with children will be explored in Chapter 5.

Every Child Matters and building positive relationships with children

The table below looks at the lunchtime supervisor's role in supporting the five *ECM* outcomes by building positive relationships with children.

ECM outcomes	The ways the lunchtime supervisor can support the five *ECM* outcomes by building positive relationships with children
Be healthy	Contribute to the social and emotional development of pupils by: Listening and mediating Helping children to deal with and express their feelings Building children's self-esteem by offering genuine praise Developing trusting relationships Providing a positive role model Encouraging children to be physically active Encouraging healthy eating

Stay safe	Ensuring safe and positive behaviour
	Listening when children talk about bullying or abuse
	Encouraging children to be assertive and to stand up for themselves
	Helping children to deal with conflict constructively
Enjoy and achieve	Encouraging children to interact and participate
	Providing a positive eating environment
	Promote structured and unstructured activities
	Encourage inclusion of all pupils
	Make lunchtime fun
Make a positive contribution	Encourage inclusion of all pupils
	Help all pupils to participate in a range of activities
	Support communication skills (their views and their emotions)
	Ensure pupils are consulted on issues that affect them
	Help children to support each other
	Encourage negotiation, co-operation, and empathy
	Help children to understand fairness and how to be a responsible citizen
	Help children to problem-solve and tackle difficulties
	Encourage children to reflect on and learn from their actions
Achieve economic wellbeing	Encourage leadership and independence
	Empower children to contribute ideas and initiatives
	Encourage children to aim high and believe in themselves.

Conclusion

In this chapter many of the necessary skills to develop relationships have been explored, and some of the potential difficulties have been outlined. Human relationships are complex and there will be no easy formula or 'magic wand' to wave to guarantee success. There is always more to learn, and we constantly develop by watching others, by talking to colleagues and by thinking about how our actions can be improved. Children will forgive us if we occasionally get things wrong, as long as we show them that we are trying our best and that we are committed to their wellbeing.

Further information

Consulting pupils – see *Working Together: Listening to the Voices of Children and Young People* (DCSF 2008).

Burnham, L. and Jones, H. (2002) *The Teaching Assistant's Handbook.* Oxford: Heinemann.

Encouraging positive behaviour in the playground and in the dining room

Introduction

LTSs are responsible for managing behaviour and keeping children safe. It is easy to underestimate how difficult this can be. After a structured morning in the classroom, young children appear to be programmed to run, shout, climb (anything including the spiked fence!), splash in puddles, kick anything, and throw objects no matter what the shape or size. You will often be required to stop them doing what they particularly enjoy, and in this the seeds of conflict can be sown.

In the past, misbehaviour was dealt with by threat of, or use of, physical punishment and humiliation. In schools today we try to understand why children misbehave and to help them to learn the consequences of their actions. We also encourage them to become well-balanced, self-disciplined human beings. Effective behaviour management depends on having skilled staff working together, using a range of agreed strategies in a well-organised environment.

There is never a single correct way to manage behaviour, as every school and child will be different and every adult will have their own unique way of doing things. There are, however, methods that can be particularly effective. This chapter starts by exploring the reasons why children misbehave. It will then summarise some of the theories that have influenced behaviour management, and will outline a range of ways to encourage children to behave positively.

Why children misbehave

When considering how best to encourage children to behave, it is helpful to have some understanding of the reasons underlying their misbehaviour.

ACTIVITY 1

In groups, write down a quick list of reasons why children misbehave. Compare your list with your colleagues'.

Children are born with individual personalities and temperaments that can affect the way they conduct themselves.

Reasons for misbehaviour may include the child:

- Being unmotivated due to low self-esteem
- Experiencing family problems/crises
- Being the subject of abuse or harsh parenting
- Reacting to peer pressure or bullying
- Reacting to the high or low expectations of others
- Finding the work too difficult or too easy
- Feeling unwell, hungry, thirsty, hot, tired, over-excited, or responding to 'raging hormones'
- Being from a different culture, with language difficulties or different expectations
- Having special educational needs, disability or medical problems
- 'Testing' to see how far they can go
- Attention-seeking or bidding for power
- Reacting to unclear or inconsistent rules and expectations
- Responding to poor teaching
- Reacting to pressures due to school tests, for example SATS.

The following case studies demonstrate reasons for misbehaviour and show how the LTS's understanding helped.

CASE STUDY 1

A child displayed disobedient behaviour following the death of a close family member. Once the LTS understood this, they were more able to respond to her in a caring rather than punishing way.

CASE STUDY 2

A child became agitated when the LTS insisted that he look at her when she was talking. The LTS remembered that in certain cultures direct eye contact can be seen as confrontational and was able to amend her request.

CASE STUDY 3

An LTS noticed that a junior school child would not do as she asked when with her friends. The LTS was aware of the power of peer pressure and decided to remove the audience of children.

ACTIVITY 2

Think of examples of factors that you have taken into account when managing children's behaviour.

How have you adapted your interventions in the light of these factors?

A theory to explain children's misbehaviour

Rudolf Dreikurs, a psychologist, maintained that children misbehave as an unhelpful way to try to meet their needs and to find acceptance within the family or group. He described how misbehaviour is often based on their mistaken beliefs about themselves and others. We need to help children to understand their behaviour, and find better ways to meet their needs. Dreikurs *et al.* (1998) described four categories of children who misbehave.

1 Attention-seekers

Some children have learnt that if they misbehave they will be given lots of attention, which they possibly fail to get in other areas of their lives. Dreikurs believed that 90 per cent of all misbehaviour is for attention. In response, many schools try to reward positive behaviour and, whenever possible, to remove attention from the negative behaviour.

2 Power seekers

Such children appear to need to have the last word, to dominate and to win. When working with them, you are likely to feel challenged or threatened, with the desire to 'make them do as they are told'. The misbehaviour is likely to continue when the child is challenged. This group also plays to an audience. In response, you will need to find ways to defuse the power battle. Such strategies will be discussed later in Chapter 5.

3 Revenge seekers

This group of children believe that they have been badly treated in life and so attempt to get their own back on others. The target of the revenge may be teachers, LTSs or other children, and sometimes this can result in bullying behaviour. Ways to help these children are outlined in Chapter 6, which tackles bullying.

4 Children who feel inadequate

These children have become discouraged and have given up. They believe they are not as good as others and have no chance of succeeding or belonging, so fail to join in to avoid further humiliation or embarrassment. Such children can be difficult to engage with and are unlikely to ask for help. Strategies of praise and reward can be helpful.

ACTIVITY 3

Can you think of children with whom you work who fit into the above groups?

When dealing with their behaviour, what has worked?

Can you think of occasions when you have helped children to understand their behaviour and to think about how they could do things differently?

Theories that have influenced the way schools manage children's behaviour

Did you know?

The following are some of the most popular theories that are likely to have influenced the way schools manage behaviour.

The Behaviourist Theory (B.F. Skinner)

B.F Skinner, in the 1940s, described how animals and humans learn to repeat behaviour that leads to pleasure, and to avoid behaviour that results in pain. When given praise or attention for certain behaviours, children are therefore likely to repeat this behaviour, as praise and attention are pleasurable. Giving such praise is known as positive reinforcement. Punishment is unpleasant and so it is likely that behaviour that is punished or ignored will decrease.

The Social Learning Theory (Albert Bandura)

Social learning focuses on how learning occurs in a social situation, when we observe others and model ourselves upon them in an attempt to gain reward, praise, acceptance or pleasure. Children therefore need to be given lots of opportunities to see others being successful, and to be encouraged to believe that they can be successful too. The social learning theorists outline the importance of peer pressure and the powerful effect of positive role models (summary of Ormond's Psychology of Learning, 2000).

Self-fulfilling Prophecy and Labelling Theory (Merton, Rosenthal and Becker)

This theory suggests that children will be influenced by the way in which others view them. Children want approval, so when we communicate the belief that they are good, the child is likely to believe in themselves and to behave in a desirable way. If we communicate the belief that they are bad or naughty, the child is likely to see themselves as bad and live up to those expectations. In such circumstances children are being labelled *good* or *bad*, and these labels are likely to stick and to become *self-fulfilling prophecies.* For example: 'I believe I am bad and so I will behave in a bad way'. I will then be told I am bad. Ways to avoid this vicious circle will be discussed later in the chapter.

Bill Rogers – a rights and responsibility model (The 4 Rs)

Bill Rogers proposes a 4R model which is popular in schools today. He describes how using the ideas of *rights, responsibilities, rules* and *routines* can help to manage behaviour. For example, all pupils have the *right* to feel safe in school, the *right* to learn, the right to be treated with respect and dignity. These rights need to be balanced with *responsibilities.* For example, all pupils are *responsible* for letting others learn. Schools need clear *rules* and consequences to protect the rights of others. For example 'if you disrupt the lesson you are interfering with other people's right to learn, and so you will miss playtime'. The *routines* are the way schools organise things. For example, how children are expected to line up in the dining room. Bill Rogers outlines a range of strategies to encourage acceptable behaviour based on communicating clear expectations. He also describes how we can manage behaviour in a way that keeps conflict to a minimum. This will be discussed below and in Chapter 5.

Culturally sensitive behaviour management (Lalit Kumar 1991)

This theory outlines the importance of understanding how social ideas, values and standards of behaviour may differ depending on a person's culture. Behaviour that we do not initially understand, and which we may see as problematic, is more likely to make sense when viewed in its cultural context. For example, in some societies males are unwilling to recognise female authority. This may explain why some male children ignore requests made by female LTSs.

Lalit Kumar describes how, when working in a multicultural community, to avoid miscommunication, schools need to understand the specific meaning of children's body language and non-verbal communication. The use of eye contact is an interesting example. In western society we see the lack of eye contact as a sign of rudeness, whilst Asian or Japanese pupils may look away from adults as a sign of respect. Black Caribbean pupils are more likely to see prolonged eye contact as confrontational. Hand gestures and facial expressions are also easily misunderstood. For example, in some cultures people tend to smile or laugh when under pressure, which may be mistakenly viewed as rudeness rather than anxiety.

Ways to encourage children's positive behaviour – a whole school model

There are many other important ways to encourage children to behave positively. These involve all school staff including LTSs.

- Being firm, fair and consistent
- Having high expectations for all pupils
- Focusing on what you would like children to do rather than on what you would not like them to do
- Planning for good behaviour
- Offering praise and reward
- Separating and responding to behaviour without condemning the child
- Using your understanding of why children misbehave (see case studies on pages 37–8)
- Encouraging children to take responsibility for their own behaviour
- Being an effective role model
- Considering the importance of physical and environmental issues.

Each of these points will be discussed below.

Being firm, fair and consistent

When staff members work together in a firm, fair and consistent way, children are more likely to behave well. They will feel secure and clear about your expectations. They will also be unable to play one team member off against another, or LTSs off against teaching staff. This is known as a whole school approach to behaviour management. To achieve consistency, schools will require clear channels of communication and a strong, well written behaviour policy. This is outlined in greater detail in Chapter 5 and in the notes for managers for this chapter.

LTSs will also need to demonstrate to children that they are prepared to: do what they say, avoid making promises they can't keep, be fair and listen to both side of the story, offer explanations for their requests and adapt their decisions when appropriate.

Have high expectations for all pupils

LTSs should have high expectations of all pupils and communicate these clearly. To do this assertively you will need to develop a sense of authority, which often comes from a belief in one's own abilities. Without having to shout, nag or threaten, you can learn to convey the message, 'This is what I expect, and I have no doubt that you will do it'.

Ways to communicate your expectations

LTSs describe a range of ways in which they communicate their expectations without resorting to shouting. Many believe shouting at children is counter-productive and that everyone just gets louder. By shouting you also risk frightening small children and losing their respect.

Having an agreed range of non-verbal signals

LTSs may use a range of agreed non-verbal signals to communicate their expectations to children. These often involve the use of hand gestures, which children may be required to copy. For example, rather than shouting, you may use this method to signal that you want quiet in the dining room. This is most effective when the whole school community use the same signals to communicate their expectations and when it is consistently reinforced.

ACTIVITY 4

In small groups think of someone at work who clearly communicates their high expectations in relation to children's behaviour.

Describe how they do this, considering their body language, their tone of voice and any other relevant factors.

Some of your answers may include:

- The person's body language backs up the words they use. For example, they stand 'tall and firm' when giving an instruction
- They appear to mean what they say, and expect others to co-operate
- Their tone of voice is clear, low and firm
- They use words that are understood by the children
- Their sentences are short and to the point
- They speak slowly and pause, repeating instructions when necessary
- They give clear instructions about what they want to happen, rather than what they don't want to happen.

The person you have selected may be a teacher or senior manager, and although their status might give them greater authority, you too can learn to communicate in this way.

The use of body language, facial expressions and tone of voice have already been discussed in Chapter 3. Without having to say a word, LTSs describe how they can communicate approval or disapproval just by looking. This has been playfully named 'the look', and in a training session an LTS amused the group by describing how a small child asked her, 'Why are you telling me off with your eyes?'

When considering your voice, bear in mind that it can help to lower it and slow down the pace when you are aiming to give instructions. You may also need to speak fairly loudly, without shouting. By using fewer words, with pauses, you can actually help to keep the child's attention. Similarly, repeating the main part of your instruction slowly and clearly may help to show that you mean what you say. This is known as assertive communication.

ACTIVITY 5

In pairs, take turns to role play (act) how you could assertively ask a group of children to stop playing and to line up for dinner. Think about: your use of words, tone of voice, how quickly you speak and the number of times you paused or repeated the instruction. Also think about your body language and facial expression. Take turns to offer your partner feedback about what they did well and what could be improved.

It also makes all the difference when your authority is backed by other staff members. This has been explored in Chapter 5 and in Notes for managers, page 135.

Focus on what you would like children to do, rather than what you would like them not to do

When managing behaviour we often say things like 'Don't run' or 'Don't forget'. The use of too many don'ts can sound 'naggy' and tends to switch children off. For example, a child may be holding their dinner tray with one hand and tipping it dangerously. You are concerned that they are going to drop the food so respond by shouting 'don't drop it'. Alternatively, you could say, 'hold the tray carefully'. Although this is a little clearer, it assumes that the child's understanding of the words 'hold it carefully' is the same as yours. Children are most likely to do as asked if we describe in detail what we would like them to do. For example, in the above incident you could say: 'Hold your tray with two hands and make sure it is straight'. This leaves little doubt about what is being requested.

ACTIVITY 6

Fill in column 3 with a description of what you could say to a child to explain what you would like them to do. The first example has been filled in to help you.

The behaviour	Your usual response	Description of what you want to happen
A child is balancing dangerously on a climbing frame	Be careful, you'll fall!	I want to see both feet on the bar please, and hold on with both hands.
A child is walking towards the road	Don't go in the road!	
A child is shouting when telling you what happened	Stop shouting please!	
A child is bossing the others around	Don't be so bossy!	

Possible answers:

- Stay on the pavement
- Speak quietly please
- Try to take turns to decide.

Planning for good behaviour

Effective management of behaviour involves planning for good behaviour rather than reacting when things go wrong. This involves thinking about the potential behavioural problems at lunchtime, and planning to avoid them. For example, you may know which children wind each other up in the dining room, and so you can ensure they do not sit together. You may notice that playground behaviour becomes particularly difficult 15 minutes before the end of the lunch hour, when large numbers of children are out in the playground, and so you can decide to introduce a period of structured games to re-focus their energy. Your team will need time to plan together how best to achieve these improvements and to discuss them with your line manager. Planning for good behaviour can also include being positive, giving lots of praise and thinking about ways to avoid confrontation. These will be explored in greater detail below and in the next chapter.

ACTIVITY 7

Can you think of other examples of how you have anticipated difficulties and planned to avoid them?

Offering praise and reward

Some theorists would suggest that we need to praise children at least six times more than we tell them off, as giving attention to behaviour (either good or bad) will result in it being repeated. The praise offered needs to be genuine, otherwise children will sense your insincerity. The value of offering descriptive praise has been discussed in the previous chapter.

Catch them being good

Even when children have a tendency to misbehave regularly, it is helpful to 'catch them being good' and to praise them for it. This is demonstrated by the case study below.

CASE STUDY 4

An LTS described a particularly disruptive boy in year 5 who had family problems. He seemed to thrive on being told off, as a way to get himself noticed. The LTS struggled to find behaviour to praise, but along with teaching staff made a decision to focus on even the smallest piece of positive behaviour. They decided to praise him when he queued up quietly for lunch or shared playground equipment with others. In time, the positive behaviour became more frequent and their relationships gradually improved.

Systems used to reward positive behaviour

Schools often have systems which use this principle. For example, staff may be encouraged to comment on the children who *are* lining up well or putting away their playground equipment, rather than focusing on the children who are not. A smile or a thumbs up, as well as verbal praise, can work wonders, particularly with younger children who often join in with the desired behaviour to earn your approval.

Schools may also introduce reward systems where stickers, house points or certificates are given at lunchtime, as well as during the day, for good behaviour or effort. A 'table of the week' may be created, where the best behaved group of children sits at a decorated table at lunchtime and is awarded extra privileges. These systems need to be linked with the whole school behaviour policy and reviewed regularly. Many LTSs believe these schemes can be extremely helpful, although some find them difficult to implement fairly. There is often a concern that the quiet, well behaved children tend to be overlooked.

ACTIVITY 8

Think of the times you have encouraged good behaviour by giving children praise or reward. What sorts of behaviour do you praise?

Observe your practice over the next few days. How often do you offer praise and how often do you tell children off? Are you happy with this balance?

Can you think of times when you have given pupils' unacceptable behaviour lots of attention?

What systems do you have at lunchtime to reward positive behaviour?

What could improve these systems?

Separate and respond to a child's behaviour without condemning the child

As already outlined in this chapter, if we label children, it is likely to affect the way they feel and behave. Even as adults we can often remember the labels we were given as children. When correcting children, it is more helpful to comment on the behaviour we wish to change. For example, if a child hurts another you can say, 'that was an unkind thing *to do*', rather than, 'you are an unkind girl'. By focusing on the behaviour, you are less likely to damage the child's self-esteem and will give the message that a child can behave differently next time. Children are very quick to imitate adults and to label each other. This behaviour needs to be challenged, too.

ACTIVITY 9

Can you remember the labels you were given as a child?

How do you think these labels have affected you in adult life?

Encouraging children to take responsibility for their own behaviour

This can be done by:

- Involving them in drawing up playground and dining room rules
- Requesting feedback about how they experience the rules at lunchtime and encouraging suggestions for improvements
- Discussing behaviour issues with children whenever possible. It is sometimes helpful to ask a child what they would do if they were you
- Teaching children basic conflict resolution skills by encouraging them to discuss their difficulties and come to their own solutions. This has been discussed further in Chapter 3
- Encouraging them to become involved with lunchtime schemes and initiatives.

Being an effective role model

As discussed in Chapter 3, the way you behave at work will demonstrate to children how you expect them to behave. They will learn a great deal by seeing how you act towards them and others. Some of the important qualities to model include: calmness, predictability, politeness, tolerance, listening skills and how to resolve conflict.

Considering physical and environmental issues

Many physical and environmental factors will affect children's behaviour. LTSs describe how on windy days 'all hell is likely to break loose'. If children are bored, hungry, thirsty, hot and bothered, full of food additives or uncomfortable, tempers are more likely to flare.

If the dining room is unattractive, noisy and the queues are long, behaviour is likely to deteriorate. The state of the toilets is important, as research suggests that large numbers of children will refuse to use them if they are dirty or smelly, and so may spend their day in discomfort.

Schools respond to these difficulties by providing breakfast clubs and water fountains, pagodas or other shade-giving constructions in the playground. There is not a lot you can do about windy days!

Every Child Matters and encouraging positive behaviour

The table below looks at the lunchtime supervisor's role in supporting the five *ECM* outcomes when encouraging positive behaviour in the playground and dining room.

ECM outcomes	The lunchtime supervisor's role in supporting the five *ECM* outcomes when encouraging positive behaviour in the dining room and the playground
Be healthy	Contribute to the children's social and emotional development Build children's self-esteem by offering praise and being fair Separate the behaviour from the child, so sustaining self-esteem Help children to resolve conflict, problem-solve and manage their feelings Provide a positive role model
Stay safe	Set clear but fair limits Have high expectations and plan for positive behaviour Teach children to deal with conflict constructively Encourage children to be assertive and stand up for themselves Display zero tolerance towards bullying and violence or antisocial behaviour
Enjoy and achieve	Provide clear praise and rewards for positive behaviour Provide a positive and enjoyable lunchtime experience Encourage inclusion and independence for all pupils Ensure the indoor and outdoor environment is as comfortable and stimulating as possible

Make a positive contribution	Ensure pupils are consulted regularly and offer feedback on issues that affect them
	Encourage children to understand their own behaviour and to develop strategies to manage emotions
	Encourage children to contribute to developing lunchtimes rules for behaviour
	Help children to support each other and develop positive relationships
	Encourage children to take responsibility for their own behaviour
	Help children to problem-solve and tackle difficulties
	Encourage children to reflect on and take responsibility for their actions
Achieve economic wellbeing	Encourage leadership, independence and teamwork
	Encourage pupils to support and lead lunchtime activities
	Empower children to initiate and develop schemes to promote positive behaviour
	Encourage children to aim high.

Conclusion

If you are able to successfully encourage children to behave well, you are less likely to have to deal with difficult and challenging incidents. A number of strategies and skills have been outlined above. In the next chapter, ways to deal with unacceptable behaviour will be explored.

Further information and reading

Dreikurs, Rudolf, Grunwald, Bernice and Pepper, Floy (1998) *Maintaining Sanity in the Classroom: Classroom Management Techniques.* New York: Taylor and Francis.

Kumar, Lalit (1991) *Teaching in England: Awareness of Different Cultural Traits.* Teachernet website.

Rogers, Bill (2003) *Behaviour Management: A Whole School Approach.* London: Paul Chapman.

Tauber, Robert T. (1997) *Self-fulfilling Prophecy: A Practical Guide to its Use in Education.* Portsmouth, NH: Greenwood Publishing Group.

Theory into practice database – http://tip.psychology.org/behaviourism

Managing unacceptable behaviour at lunchtime

Introduction

Dealing with unacceptable behaviour is often the area that LTSs are most keen to discuss. Perhaps they secretly hope they will learn the magic answers to achieve a perfect lunchtime full of well-behaved children. Unfortunately, these answers do not exist, and perfectly behaved children do not exist either. However, there are skills, strategies and whole school practices that can help you

This chapter starts by exploring a whole school model of behaviour management. Effective strategies to deal with unacceptable behaviour will then be examined. The chapter concludes by focusing on dealing with challenges, including verbal abuse and violence, dining room rules and guidance for wet play. These can be displayed and referred to regularly.

Having clear and consistent consequences in response to misbehaviour

Your school will need to agree on consequences for unacceptable behaviour. Sanctions may include: time out, the loss of privileges, being reported verbally or in writing, or, for more serious incidents, being sent to a senior manager to be dealt with. Sanctions need to be seen

as a logical consequence of the pupil's inappropriate behaviour. They should never be humiliating or degrading. They should be implemented consistently at playtime, lunchtime and during the rest of the school day.

The law

The Education and Inspection Act 2006 requires that head teachers *must* determine measures on behaviour and discipline that form the school's behaviour policy. Measures, in this context, include rules, rewards, sanctions, and behaviour-management strategies. The policy determined by the head teacher must include measures to be taken with a view to 'encouraging good behaviour and respect for others on the part of pupils and, in particular, preventing all forms of bullying among pupils'.

The Act outlines how all teachers and other staff in charge of pupils have the power to discipline, but the head teacher may limit the power to apply particular sanctions to certain staff.

Agreement is needed amongst the whole staff team about:

- What type of behaviour warrants particular sanctions
- Who has the power to implement particular sanctions
- When behaviour must be reported, and how this is to be done
- How many warnings the child should be given before action is taken
- How long the punishment should last
- What will happen next if the behaviour does not improve
- Who will follow up on reported incidents
- How can you obtain feedback on how reported incidents have been dealt with.

The use of 'time out' as a sanction

Many schools have special places in the playground (often a bench or a wall) where children can be sent to for a few minutes to calm down and to 'think about their behaviour'. This cooling-off period also removes the child from a difficult situation. There may also be a supervised indoor place within the school where children can be sent as a punishment for more serious offences. As already discussed, it is important when using sanctions, to keep the focus on the child's behaviour and to remind them that you expect better of them in the future.

Strategies for challenging unacceptable behaviour

This section will focus on skills and strategies which individuals and teams can use to challenge unacceptable behaviour. There is no easy way to make children behave. What works for one person may not work for another and what works on one day may not work the next. Successful behaviour management is like having a bag of tricks and knowing how to select the most effective one for a particular situation.

Behaviour that particularly winds you up

Managing children's behaviour can stir up powerful feelings. We are all likely to find some behaviour difficult to cope with, and it is not unusual for children to sense our weak spots and to push us to the limit. Knowing what winds you up, and if possible why it does so, may help you to react in a calmer and less emotional way.

ACTIVITY 1

Discuss in pairs:

What behaviour really 'gets you going'?

How does it make you feel?

What would you like to say or do to the child responsible for the behaviour?

The behaviour usually listed includes:

- Rudeness/attitude
- Swearing
- Violence
- Bullying
- Being ignored
- Children making rude faces, mimicking you or giggling behind your back.

When dealing with unacceptable behaviour, you will need to make decisions about when and how best to challenge the child.

Types of challenges

Challenging children's behaviour respectfully can help them to learn what is socially acceptable. Being harsh or aggressive can be counter-productive and may distress sensitive or younger children. Types of challenges include:

Explaining what you would like to happen and why

For example: a child splashes in a puddle in the playground, and you say, 'I would like you to move away from the puddle or you will get wet and have to sit in wet clothes all afternoon'. This informs the child what you would like to happen and what the consequences will be if the behaviour continues. It is not unusual to have to repeat such requests on many occasions.

The use of warnings and consequences

If your request for change has been unsuccessful, you may decide to introduce a warning and a consequence. The warning acts to give the child a choice. For example, 'If you don't stop splashing, I will have to report you – it's up to you'. If the child does not do as instructed, you will need to follow through with your threat and report him or her.

Firm challenges when there is violence or danger

When responding to violence or danger, you will need to challenge a child assertively, often without giving an explanation. For example, if she is climbing on to the roof, you are likely to say in a firm, calm and strong voice: 'Get down now', and to discuss the reasons when the child is safely on the ground.

The 'broken record'

This type of challenge can be used when you have already given an explanation for your instruction. For example, you have asked a child to come off the climbing frame and have explained why. She refuses and starts to argue, so you repeat the statement a number of times in a calm and firm manner (as if the record has got stuck): 'I want you to get down now'. The child will know by your tone and by the repetition of the instruction that you are not going to change your mind. If this is not working, you will need to try another method, possibly a warning followed by a consequence.

Strategies you can use to reduce the risk of confrontation

Bill Rogers describes the importance of managing behaviour in a way that keeps power struggles and confrontation to the minimum.

Some of his strategies include:

- Responding to incidents that matter
- Keeping the focus on the primary behaviour
- Tactically ignoring
- Partial agreement
- Distraction
- Using the language of choice.

These will now be discussed.

Responding to incidents that matter

When managing behaviour, it is important to know when to decide to let things go. In other words it helps to pick your battles. This is not a case of being too lazy to tackle difficulties, but more a case of deciding what matters and dealing with it consistently and effectively. For example, if a child makes a silly face behind your back, you may decide to let this go. This is known as *tactical ignoring*. You should never ignore behaviour that is violent, unsafe, racist or seriously insulting to you or to others.

Keeping the focus on the primary behaviour

You see a child throwing earth at another child in the playground. You challenge him firmly and he responds in an angry way: 'Why are you picking on me? I wasn't the only one throwing earth. It's not fair'. In this situation the throwing of the earth is the *primary* behaviour and the child's angry response when challenged is the *secondary* behaviour, which is his way of defending himself, appearing cool in front of friends or distracting you. Secondary behaviour can also take the form of being rude, aggressive body language or having the clever last word. Rather than going into attack and engaging in a power struggle with the child, it is far more useful to keep the focus on the primary behaviour (your initial challenge about throwing earth) by saying something like: 'Maybe you weren't the only one throwing earth, but I saw you throw it and I want you to stop now and move away from the grass'. If the child answers back, rudely, rather than getting sucked into a full-scale argument, continue to comment on the earth throwing and what you would like to happen.

Tactical ignoring

As described above, tactically ignoring involves a decision to ignore behaviour for a particular reason. For example, a child may be messing around in the queue, knowing that this is a great way to get your attention. You make a decision to ignore him completely, and to focus your attention on the children on either side who are standing quietly. It would be inappropriate to ignore safety issues, aggression, violence, bullying or serious incidents.

Partial agreement

In the above earth throwing incident, the response given to the child included the words 'Maybe you weren't the only one throwing earth, but...'. This is an example of a *partial agreement*. By agreeing with *some* of what the child has said, you are showing that you are prepared to meet them half way. This can have a calming effect, which then allows you both to focus on the original behaviour.

Distraction

In some situations you may decide to distract a child who is misbehaving. For example, when a child is making rude faces behind your back, you may decide to ignore this and to distract him or her by encouraging them to help you to collect the playground equipment. By doing so you are refusing to rise to the bait, whilst also engaging them in a constructive activity.

Using the language of choice

Imagine you are in the playground and you see a child drop a piece of litter. When asked, he or she refuses to pick it up. You are now faced with a decision about how best to gain the pupil's co-operation without making the situation worse. You might try to appeal to the child's better nature by saying in a friendly way 'please help me and pick up the paper', or you might turn it into a game and suggest that you pick it up together. We cannot *make* the child do something that they are refusing to do. Giving them a limited choice can, however, take the heat out of the situation and result in a positive outcome. This is illustrated in the examples below.

CASE STUDY 1

When the child refuses to pick up the litter, you could give him or her limited choice by saying, 'I do want you to pick up the paper. Would you like to do it now or in one minute?'. This gives the child some say in the matter and so they no longer feel 'cornered', or that they have to fight to win. It is amazing how often the child backs down with the sense that they have not lost face.

CASE STUDY 2

A child continues to play with some equipment, when you have told him to put it away. Instead of physically removing it, you could give him a limited choice by saying, 'I want you to put that in the box. Would you like to do it yourself or would you prefer me to do it?' The choice gives the child some control and makes it more likely that he will do as asked. If the child does not respond to your first choice, you can give another choice: 'Either you do as I asked or I will have to put your name in the behaviour book; it's up to you'.

In some schools the language of choice is used on an everyday basis as part of the behaviour policy. Staff are encouraged to ask children if they have made 'good' or 'bad' choices as a way of helping them to consider their actions.

When managing behaviour it is helpful to practise using a range of methods. None of the above will work every time, but if you have a number of options to pick from you are far more likely to be successful.

ACTIVITY 2

How many of the above strategies have you used at work? You may need to remind yourself of these by reading the relevant paragraphs above. Fill in columns 2 and 3.

Type of strategy	Do you use it?	Give an example of how you have used this strategy
	Yes / No	
Challenging with an explanation	☐ / ☐	....
Using a warning followed by a consequence	☐ / ☐	....
Firm challenges when there is violence or danger	☐ / ☐	....
The 'broken record'	☐ / ☐	....
Using the language of choice	☐ / ☐	....
Respond to incidents that matter	☐ / ☐	....
Keep the focus on the primary behaviour	☐ / ☐	....
Tactical ignoring	☐ / ☐	....
Partial agreement	☐ / ☐	....

Consider the behaviour management case studies below. Try to be as flexible as possible and think of a number of ways to deal with each problem.

ACTIVITY 3

Behaviour management case studies:

What strategies would you try in the following situations and why?

1 You see a boy on the flat roof of the school dining hall about to rescue a ball. He refuses to come down when you tell him to.

2 There is a commotion on one of the tables in the dining room. When you go over you find that children have been flicking peas at each other. There are eight children on the table. It is not clear how many of them have been involved.

3 When you tell a child to line up she says, 'My mum says you can't make me – you are just the dinner lady'.

4 You see a child drop a wrapper on the floor and ask her to pick it up. She says, 'No – why should I?'.

5 There is a puddle in the playground and you explain why they should not get wet. The children continue splashing in it as soon as your back is turned.

6   A group of children call a group of Muslim children racist names.

7   A child, well known for having a short fuse, has lost his temper following an argument with another child. You want him to calm down before discussing his behaviour.

8   You see a group of year 6 children giggle and make faces behind your back.

Coping with the most challenging behaviour

At the start of Chapter 4, the complex reasons for misbehaviour were discussed briefly. For some children, their difficulties may be so great that they regularly resort to unmanageable, violent or extremely abusive behaviour. No matter how expert or skilful you may be, this behaviour is likely to remain problematic. Often these are the children that others are struggling to manage, and it is important not to see their misbehaviour as your personal failure.

Special arrangements that can be helpful

Lunchtime can be a particularly challenging time for some troubled children, and it may help to make some special arrangements.

An LTS described how her school had developed an extremely successful indoor lunchtime club where some of the most troubled children were required to attend on a daily basis. The children were gradually allowed back into the playground on a part-time basis when they felt able to cope and to behave.

When working with such children, you are likely to need regular back-up and support from teaching staff or other involved experts. This may mean that a senior manager joins you in the playground or that children can be taken into school when necessary.

At one school the LTS requested walkie-talkies to be used in emergencies to summon help. Another school developed a red card system where children were given a card to take into the school which signalled the need for immediate back-up.

Schools often draw up individual behaviour plans which outline the school's expectations and targets for particular children to meet. You may find it helpful to meet with the SENCO or class teacher to share relevant information and practice.

Physical contact and restraint

During lunchtime you have a responsibility to keep children safe. However, it is crucial that you do not hurt a child in your attempt to protect others, or when you have lost your temper. Section 93 of the Education and Inspections Act 2006 enables school staff to use *such force as is reasonable* in certain circumstances.

As outlined in the DCSF's 'The use of force to control or restrain pupils: non-statutory guidance for schools in England 2007':

> There may be occasions where it is necessary for staff to restrain a pupil physically to prevent them from inflicting injury to others, self-injury, damaging property, or causing disruption. In such cases only the minimum force necessary may be used and any action taken must be to restrain the pupil. Where an employee has taken action to physically restrain a pupil they should make a written report of the incident in the form prescribed by the school's policy on restraint.

Guidance for Safer Working Practice for Adults who Work with Children and Young People (DCSF 2007) states that:

This means that adults working with children should:

- adhere to the organisation's physical intervention policy
- always seek to defuse situations
- always use minimum force for the shortest period necessary
- record and report as soon as possible after the event any incident where physical intervention has been used.

This means that organisations should:

- have a policy on the use of physical intervention in place that complies with government guidance and legislation and describes the context in which it is appropriate to use physical intervention
- ensure that an effective recording system is in place which allows for incidents to be tracked and monitored
- ensure adults are familiar with the above
- ensure that staff are appropriately trained.

Schools are advised to create their own policy on the use of reasonable force to control or restrain pupils and issues to consider include breaking up fights at lunchtime. Support staff should not restrain pupils without having learned how to do so. Many education authorities offer training in this area. Your head teacher is ultimately responsible for how much physical contact support staff use, which must be reasonable in the circumstances. It is important that you receive guidance.

When you have been hurt or verbally abused

Unfortunately, it is not unusual for LTSs to be hit, kicked and verbally or racially abused by pupils. Such behaviour is unacceptable, and must be taken extremely seriously. On occasions, LTSs have described how they are left feeling stressed, depressed and demoralised. They tend to underplay the incident, believing it to be somehow their fault. Following such attacks, it is important that you feel able to request appropriate help, and that this is made available. This may include seeking an apology from the child and seeing evidence that the school is taking appropriate action.

Behaving professionally and looking after yourself

Managing challenging behaviour can generate powerful negative feelings. When working with challenging children relationships can be volatile. As the adult, you will need to show them that you do not bear a grudge and that you are ready to rebuild the relationship. You may feel able to apologise if you have lost your temper, or to explain how angry the child's behaviour has made you.

Every Child Matters when managing unacceptable behaviour

The table below looks at the lunchtime supervisor's role in supporting the five *ECM* outcomes when managing unacceptable behaviour.

ECM outcomes	The lunchtime supervisor's role in supporting the five ECM outcomes when managing unacceptable behaviour
Be healthy	Support and contribute to pupil's behaviour by implementing a range of appropriate strategies
	Separate the behaviour from the child, so sustaining self-esteem.
	Help children to resolve conflict, problem solve and manage their feelings
	Provide a positive role model
Stay safe	Set clear but fair limits
	Support children in behaving safely and responsibly
	Prevent children harming themselves or others by their actions
	Teach children to deal with conflict constructively
	Follow school guidelines in relation to physical contact and restraining pupils
	Display zero tolerance towards bullying and violence, racism or antisocial behaviour
Enjoy and achieve	Encourage children to take responsibility for their own behaviour
	Provide clear praise and rewards for positive behaviour
	Contribute to a positive dining room and playground environment
	Plan for stimulating and well organised lunchtime and wet play
Make a positive contribution	Ensure pupils are regularly consulted and offer feedback on issues that affect them
	Encourage children to understand their own behaviour and to develop strategies to manage emotions
	Encourage children to contribute to developing lunchtime rules for behaviour
	Help children to problem solve, tackle difficulties and reflect on and take responsibility for their actions
	Encourage pupils to voice their concerns in a confident and assertive way
	Involve pupils in buddy schemes and other behaviour initiatives
Achieve economic well-being	Encourage leadership, independence and teamwork
	Empower pupils to demonstrate initiative and calculate risk when making decisions.

Conclusion

During the lunchtime break you have the challenging job of supervising a large number of children in sometimes difficult circumstances. This chapter has offered a range of strategies and whole school practices that will help you to manage children's behaviour. Do not expect to be successful all the time, and learn from the times things go wrong as well as times when things go well.

Further information and reading

DCSF (2007) *Guidance for Safer Working Practice for Adults who Work with Children and Young People.*

DCSF (2007) *The Use of force to Control or Restrain Pupils. Non-statutory Guidance for Schools in England.*

Education and Inspection Act 2006
(http://www.opsi.gov.uk/acts/acts2006/ukpga_20060040_en_1).

Physical contact (www.teachernet.gov.uk/_doc/12187/ACFD89B.pdf).

Rogers, Bill (2003) *Behaviour Management: A Whole School Approach.* London: Paul Chapman.

Dealing with bullying

Introduction

In primary schools up to three quarters of bullying is believed to take place in the playground, so LTSs have a crucial role in dealing with this problem. This includes identifying , responding to, reporting and recording incidents of bullying. You can also help children to deal with being bullied, and encourage the aggressor to behave more appropriately.

This chapter will start by exploring what constitutes bullying, who is likely to bully or be bullied, and the devastating effects it can have. The chapter will go on to look at what schools can do in response. There are no easy solutions to this problem, but by reading the chapter you will be clearer about the options available to you.

Information about bullying

What is bullying?

Bullying is when people force others, usually smaller people, to do what they want.

(Boy, year 5)

Bullying is any behaviour which is intended to hurt, threaten or frighten another person or group of people. It is difficult for those being bullied to stop the process. It involves a person or a group of people using their power over others. It is usually repetitive or persistent. It can be physical, verbal or emotional.

Pupils' understanding of bullying will vary with age. Infants may confuse bullying with frightening and nasty experiences generally, while juniors tend to develop a more mature understanding. Parents also sometimes mistakenly believe that their child is being bullied when they have argued with another child.

Forms of bullying

Young people describe how bullying can take the form of:

- Name calling or teasing
- Being threatened
- Being hit or attacked by being pushed, pulled, pinched or kicked
- Stealing others' possessions
- Being forced to do things
- Being ignored, left out or isolated by gossip and the spreading of rumours
- Cyber-bullying – receiving abusive text messages email or other types of messages on internet chatrooms.

Who gets bullied?

Some children get bullied because they are somehow different; others are bullied for no obvious reason. Research suggests that the victim may:

- Be gentle, intelligent or creative
- Lack friends
- Be a non-fighter
- Be disabled or have special needs
- Belong to an ethnic minority group, religion or be homosexual
- Be physically different although their physical characteristics may be used as an excuse by the bully
- Behave inappropriately, in a way that annoys or irritates others
- Be someone who shows their feelings
- Often believe that the bullying is their fault
- Keep what's happening secret.

The problem of racist, sexist and homophobic bullying

Prejudice exists in all races and cultures, and in a recent study, racist name-calling was found to be more common among primary than secondary school pupils, and 11 per cent of the primary pupils questioned reported that they had been called anti-gay names. Children from minority cultures and religions have historically experienced bullying, and since 9/11, Muslim children are having a particularly difficult time. Research suggests that homosexual pupils are regularly and often seriously bullied, and how both boys and girls are subjected to sexist and sexual bullying *Safe to Learn* (DCSF 2007).

Cyber-bullying

This is a growing problem. It is the use of Information Communication Technology (ICT), particularly mobile phones and the internet, deliberately to upset someone else. Although the majority of cyber-bullying takes place with older children, primary school pupils are increasingly becoming victims and perpetrators of this problem. Girls are significantly more likely to be cyber-bullied than boys.

Many young children own mobile phones and may have regular unsupervised access to the internet. At a teachers' conference, a head teacher in south London described how 'pupils as young as eight or nine are sending bullying messages to other pupils by instant messaging or emails ('Cyber bullying on the rise among primary pupils', *TES*, 21 March 2008, Jonathan Milne).

Schools often ban pupils' mobile phones or confiscate them until the end of the day. They also monitor the use of the internet and educate children about this problem.

For further information you can read *Cyberbullying – Safe to Learn: Embedding anti-bullying Work in Schools* (DCSF 2007) or *Anti-bullying Guidance for Schools*.

Who bullies?

Individuals and groups of boys are most likely to bully others, although girls bully too. Children who bully can come from a range of family backgrounds and social classes. Michelle Elliot describes how some children become 'temporary bullies' in response to a family crisis (for example, the birth of a new baby, or illness in the home). Others bully on a long-term, regular basis and some describe it as a bad habit they find difficult to break. Children who continue to bully are more likely to behave violently or criminally as adults.

Children who bully are likely to:

- Feel insecure and have low self-esteem
- Meet their needs by humiliating or dominating others
- Be scapegoats or victims in their own family
- See feelings and vulnerability as unacceptable weakness
- Lack love and limits
- Have an impulsive temperament.

(Summary from Michelle Eliot's *Keeping Safe* (1994))

The effects of bullying on children

Serious bullying can have an extremely negative impact on a child's self-esteem and quality of life. Damage can be long-term and many adults who suffered as children say they have never fully recovered. Victims may develop a range of physical and emotional symptoms. Being bullied may also lead to depression and, in the most serious cases, suicide.

(Smith 2000)

Michelle Elliot (1994), who founded the anti-bullying organisation Kidscape, describes how victims of bullying may:

- Be unwilling or frightened to go to school
- Begin to underachieve
- Become anxious and withdrawn
- Cry or have nightmares
- Have unexplained bruises or cuts
- Have possessions 'go missing'
- Refuse to say what is wrong

- Start to bully siblings
- Appear unreasonably angry with parents
- Give improbable excuses for any of the above
- Develop physical or emotional symptoms
- Self-harm or attempt or threaten suicide.

What helps children to cope with or avoid being bullied

The three most helpful factors in preventing or helping pupils to deal with, bullying are: having friends, learning to avoid the bully and learning to stand up for themselves (Thomas Coran Research Unit 2003). Fifteen per cent of the primary school pupils interviewed thought that 'hitting back' would 'always' or 'usually' work to stop bullying. Retaliating with violence is clearly discouraged by schools, but careful use of humour, changing the subject or walking away from the situation may also be effective.

What schools can do

Anti-bullying guidance for schools

Safe to Learn: Embedding Anti-bullying Work in Schools (DCSF 2007) has replaced *Bullying: Don't Suffer in Silence* as the guidelines to be followed by schools. It outlines how head teachers are required to:

- Develop measures to prevent all forms of bullying among pupils
- Publicise the measures in the behaviour policy and draw them to the attention of pupils, parents and staff at least once a year
- Determine and ensure the implementation of a policy for the pastoral care of the pupils
- Ensure the maintenance of good order and discipline at all times during the school day (including the midday break).

The legal responsibilities of governing bodies are summarised and the guidelines recommend that schools create a specialist leadership role responsible for anti-bullying work, and an anti-bullying advisory group, which includes pupils, parent and staff, to review and develop policy and practice.

In November 2008, the Department of Health and the DCSF in partnership with the Children's Commissioner and the Anti-bullying Alliance produced the *Anti-bullying Guidance for Schools*.

The SEAL programme

The SEAL programme (Social and Emotional Aspects of Learning) is often used by schools to address the problem of bullying. This is a whole school package of activities and resources that can be done in a range of settings to develop children's social and emotional skills. Many of the activities can be adapted for lunchtime, and aim to promote empathy, conflict resolution, social responsibility and assertiveness.

For further information about the programme talk to your SENCO or visit: http://nationalstrategies.standards.dcsf.gov.uk/primary/publications/banda/seal/

Healthy school status

To achieve healthy school status, schools are required to sign the DCSF Anti-Bullying Charter and use it to draw up an effective anti-bullying policy. They must also educate staff about identifying and managing bullying. Systems must be in place to report back to parents/carers on any concerns raised and for recording bullying incidents. Schools must follow up and monitor children involved in these incidents, and children and young people in school must report that they feel safe in school.

For more information visit: www.healthyschools.org.uk

The school anti-bullying policy

Schools must give clear messages that bullying is unacceptable, that immediate action will be taken by all staff, and that children should not suffer in silence. They are required to draw up procedures to prevent bullying among pupils and staff and to bring these procedures to the attention of staff, parents and pupils. The agreed policy should be written in language that everyone understands. There is now considerable emphasis on engaging pupils, staff and parents in developing, monitoring and evaluating the anti-bullying policy. Schools can develop a lunchtime anti-bullying policy which includes guidelines for LTSs. Anti-bullying practice can be reviewed regularly during meetings, INSET days and other training events.

The role of the LTS in relation to tackling bullying

To work effectively you will need to be able to:

- Identify incidents of bullying
- Make yourself open and accessible, and listen to the children
- Use school systems to ensure that information and incidents of bullying are recorded and discussed
- Work with victims of bullying and children who bully, in line with the school anti-bullying policy
- Challenge all forms of discriminatory behaviour
- Encourage bystanders to take action
- Help children to cope with friendship difficulties
- Regularly review playground organisation
- Support existing playground initiatives
- Consult with the children.

Identifying and dealing with bullying

In the first part of this chapter some of the key signs and symptoms pointing to the occurrence of bullying were outlined. When looking for bullying you are also keeping an eye on children who regularly look distressed and alone, and on children or groups of children who appear to be dominated or to be dominating others. It will help to recognise the difference between play fighting and bullying. As research by Peter Smith outlines, children's experience of bullying is often dismissed as 'play fighting' whilst on other occasions staff mistake children's rough-and-tumble play for harmful aggression. Play fighting is extremely common and can help children to acquire skills in relation to assertion and survival. When children are play fighting, you are more likely to see: smiling or laughing; 'mock' blows or kicks which do not connect, or do so only softly; children taking turns at being on top, or chasing the other. By contrast, pupils who are being attacked or physically bullied often: frown or look unhappy or angry; try to move away from the aggressor; do not take turns, as the aggressor remains dominant throughout. Both boys and girls engage in play fighting and in most cases this does not escalate into aggressive fighting. If unclear, ask participants in a friendly tone about what they are doing.

Make yourself open and accessible and listen to children

Ways to develop trusting relationships with children have been explored in Chapter 3, and you may wish to re-read parts of this chapter. Encouraging a child 'to tell' requires an adult's willingness to listen. Victims may be reluctant to tell others about bullying, feeling that it is their fault or something they have to deal with alone. Many fear that they will not be believed or that telling adults will make things worse. Children will tell you more when you listen to them in a calm, non-judgemental way and take their concerns seriously. They also need to trust that you will not tell others about the bullying unless necessary. If you will be passing incidents on to others to be dealt with, you should inform the child of this.

In the past, children were discouraged from telling tales, as they were seen to be 'snitching' or 'grassing'. Although you may sometimes feel irritated when children constantly tell on others, try to listen carefully to avoid missing something serious. It helps to find a confidential space away from friends to talk to children privately. If having listened, you do not think that the child is being bullied, discuss this with them in a sympathetic way. This leaves the door open for the child to report future incidents if necessary.

Use school systems to ensure that information and incidents of bullying are recorded and discussed

Your school is likely to have clear guidelines about the recording of incidents

In September 2008, in the *Children's Plan Progress Report*, the government announced their intention to introduce measures to ensure the proper recording of bullying within schools across the country. You will be required to communicate with teaching staff following bullying incidents at lunchtime and to record incidents in line with policy and procedures. If unclear, request clarification.

As discussed in previous chapters, sharing information is a two-way process. To be effective, it will help if you know which children are at risk of bullying or being bullied, and who is experiencing serious friendship difficulties or disputes.

ACTIVITY 1

How are you informed by other members of staff about who is bullying or who is being bullied?

Are you made aware of children's serious friendship difficulties or group disputes?

Are you clear about your school systems for recording or reporting bullying to the relevant people?

How can communication about bullying in school be improved?

Work with the victims of bullying

Your school's behaviour policy is likely to offer guidance for victims of bullying, including how to be assertive and to report bullying. LTSs can have an important role in helping children to:

- Believe that the bullying is not their fault
- Rebuild their self-esteem
- Develop strategies to cope with bullying, including assertive behaviour
- Know what action is being taken, and by whom.

Reassuring children that the bullying is not their fault

No one deserves to be bullied. Children need to be reassured that it not their fault, and that nothing is terribly wrong with them. They need to know that it was right to tell you what happened.

Help to rebuild their self-esteem

By listening, believing and supporting the child, whilst reassuring them that the bullying was not their fault, you are helping them to feel better about themselves. By encouraging children to deal with the bullying they are more likely to be able to move out of the victim role.

Help children to develop strategies to cope with bullying, including assertive behaviour

Children need to learn how to avoid the bullying and to stand up for themselves. You can ask the child what he/she would like you to do to help them, including the offer of support whilst he/she approaches and confronts the bully.

Children can learn to think, look and act assertively and you can help them to find the words to respond to being threatened, called names, excluded or hurt. Small children can practise saying 'no' or 'I don't like it when you...' or 'stop it now'. You can also encourage them to think about non-verbal communication including: hand gestures, eye contact, posture, and tone of voice. Older children will benefit from writing a diary to document the incidents, especially when bullying occurs on a regular basis.

Schools instruct children not to retaliate physically when they are attacked, although sometimes parents/carers will contradict this. No matter what you personally believe, as a member of staff you are required to accept school policy and to help children to stand up for themselves without resorting to violence.

Inform children of action being taken and by whom

Victims of bullying will be reassured by knowing that others are able to take control and deal with, or help them to deal with, the bullying. With more serious incidents you can inform the child who you will be telling, and what is likely to happen.

Work with children who bully

Your policy is likely to describe zero tolerance towards bullying. Many schools recommend that incidents are dealt with swiftly and firmly, by using a range of strategies. These are likely to include the use of sanctions such as: reprimand, detention, time out and missing treats. In the most serious cases parents may be involved and children may be excluded from school. Some schools adhere to a model of restorative justice or a 'No Blame' approach, which attempts to eliminate blame and encourage a group of children to consider ways of making things better for the victims of bullying. The group may include those directly involved as well as bystanders and, possibly, friends of the victim.

Check what sanctions you use when dealing with children who bully? Is bullying discussed by your team, the children and other staff on a regular basis?

Bullying behaviour can make us feel very angry and it is tempting for adults to 'get their own back' on the child who bullies. In fact, these children often have serious problems including low self-esteem and poor self-control, and are likely to need as much help as their victim.

When working with children who bully, it is unhelpful to label individuals with terms like 'bully' or 'troublemaker' as this could lead to further problems. You will need to find a balance between setting extremely firm limits to ensure that the behaviour stops, and helping the child to take responsibility for their actions and to cope in more constructive ways. You should be clear, honest and direct with your response, avoiding humiliation, sarcasm or aggression. By dealing with bullying in this way you are offering a positive role model. Children who bully often need to learn how to control themselves and to deal with their anger more constructively. Encourage them to develop empathy by putting themselves in the victim's shoes.

When faced with bullying behaviour, try to gain an account of what happened from the aggressor's point of view. If there is a group of children involved, it may help to talk to them individually. In the case of one-off, less serious incidents, you may impose a warning or a minor sanction. With persistent or more serious bullying you will be required to pass it to others to be dealt with. As already discussed, you are likely to benefit from discussion with the SENCO or class teacher to help you to understand the child's behaviour and the best way to deal with it.

Challenging discriminatory behaviour

You will be required to challenge racist, sexist and anti-gay bullying as well as taunts made about children who are overweight, disabled or have special educational needs. You may have to put your own personal opinions to one side and find ways to explain to children in age-appropriate language how distressing their comments and actions can be for the victim. Often small children repeat what they have heard without fully understanding the meaning of their words. Follow school guidelines for dealing with and reporting such behaviour.

Encouraging bystanders to take action

Bystanders are people who stand by and let others get picked on. They are often afraid to become involved in case they are also targeted. The majority of people act as bystanders sometimes, and schools can encourage children to take a stand in many ways.

CASE STUDY 1

One school talked about this problem in assembly and then encouraged children to role play how they could show that they disapproved when they saw others bullying someone. LTSs continued this discussion informally in the playground.

Helping children to cope with friendship difficulties

Having a group of friends has been identified as an important protective factor against bullying. However, relationships may go wrong and 20 per cent of children questioned state that their tormentor was a former friend (Thomas Coram Research Unit 2003).

LTSs can help children to deal with friendship difficulties. This means that you may have to tolerate the endless moans and complaints about who won't play with whom. Children need to be encouraged to sort out their differences without resorting to aggression or verbal abuse. Supervisors can help pupils without friends to form relationships by providing opportunities to be together and share common interests.

CASE STUDY 2

In one school, specific pupils were selected by LTSs to help with a project to improve the school grounds. Two initially friendless and bullied children, both known by a supervisor to be interested in wildlife, came together to help create a school garden.

Discuss with colleagues how you help children to develop friendships and to cope when things go wrong.

Regularly review playground organisation

There may be areas of your playground that are difficult to monitor, so keep moving and position yourself carefully. By improving the playground environment schools can reduce bullying. This will be explored in detail in Chapters 8 and 10.

Support existing playground initiatives

Playground buddy schemes involve older children befriending and supporting the younger pupils. Such schemes also have a positive effect on the whole school community and make it harder for children to stand by and let others suffer.

Consult with children on a regular basis

The government stresses the importance of involving children and young people in decision making. You can read more about this in *Are You Talking to Me? Young People's Participation in Anti-bullying: An Anti-Bullying Alliance Resource.*

Involved schools consult with staff, children and their parents on a regular basis to gauge the extent and nature of the problem of bullying. This can happen verbally or by means of a questionnaire. Schools may also have a 'help me/bully' box placed in an accessible place where concerns can be reported anonymously; think books; peer mediator schemes; confidential phone numbers or email contacts. School councils can also give input and an example of a bullying questionnaire is provided below.

Are you a boy or a girl? Boy ☐ Girl ☐

How old are you? ....

Do you understand what bullying is? Yes ☐ No ☐

Have you ever been bullied at this school? Yes ☐ No ☐

When you were bullied what happened to you?..
....

Where were you bullied?...

If you have been bullied, has it happened:

a) once? ☐ b) occasionally? ☐ c) often? ☐ d) very often? ☐

When you were bullied, who did you tell:

a) a friend? ☐ b) a parent? ☐ c) a teacher? ☐

d) nobody? ☐ e) anyone else? ☐ f) the lunchtime supervisor? ☐

Have you ever seen anyone else being bullied? Yes ☐ No ☐

When you see someone being bullied what can you do? ....
....

What would help you to feel happier and safer in the playground? ....
....

Bullying checklist for lunchtime supervisors

Consider the following questions and discuss your answers with your line manager.

Do you:	Yes	No
Know your school anti-bullying policy and follow the procedure outlined?	☐	☐
Make it clear to the children that bullying is unacceptable?	☐	☐
Share information following incidents with all relevant staff?	☐	☐
Know what to do if children are misusing mobile phones in school?	☐	☐
Record and share information following incidents with all relevant staff on a need to know basis?	☐	☐
Receive information about children to keep a special eye on?	☐	☐
Keep bullying on the agenda and encourage children to talk about it?	☐	☐
Help victims to deal with bullying?	☐	☐
Help children who bully to cope in a more constructive way?	☐	☐
Create a climate where it's acceptable to tell an adult about incidents of bullying?	☐	☐
Make yourself available to children and listen carefully to what they tell you?	☐	☐
Check and supervise all accessible areas in the playground and toilets at lunchtime?	☐	☐
Help children to cope with friendship difficulties?	☐	☐
Review playground organisation to minimise bullying?	☐	☐
Keep children constructively occupied in the playground?	☐	☐
Receive appropriate training about recognising and dealing with bullying?	☐	☐

Every Child Matters and dealing with bullying

The table below looks at the lunchtime supervisor's role in supporting the five *ECM* outcomes when dealing with bullying.

ECM outcomes	The lunchtime supervisor's role in supporting the five *ECM* outcomes when dealing with bullying
Be healthy	Help children to develop positive self-esteem by encouraging social and emotional development
	Encourage a climate of mutual respect and tolerance
	Encourage children to express their emotions without resorting to being physical
	Help children to develop empathy and understanding of differences
	Encourage children to cope with friendship disputes constructively
	Provide a positive role model in the areas outlined above
Staysafe	Set clear but fair limits in relation to behaviour
	Supervise hard-to-see areas of the playground
	Make yourself accessible and easy to talk to
	Prevent children harming or dominating others
	Teach children to deal with conflict constructively
	Encourage pupils to voice their concerns in a confident and assertive way

	Display zero tolerance towards bullying and violence, racism or antisocial behaviour
	Regularly review the playground organisation
Enjoy and achieve	Ensure all children feel clear about what to do when concerned about bullying
	Provide clear praise and rewards for positive behaviour
	Teach children strategies to deal with bullying
	Encourage respect for diversity and difference in others
Make a positive contribution	Ensure pupils are regularly consulted and can report bullying in a range of ways
	Encourage children to understand their own behaviour and to develop strategies to manage their emotions
	Encourage bystanders to act
	Encourage children to contribute to developing anti-bullying strategies
	Help children to problem solve and tackle difficulties
	Involve pupils in buddy schemes and other anti-bullying initiatives
Achieve economic wellbeing	Encourage leadership, independence and teamwork
	Empower pupils to demonstrate initiative in anti-bullying schemes.

Conclusion

LTSs have an important role in dealing with and preventing bullying. If you do this effectively you are likely to improve the lives of several of the children at school.

Finding out more

There are many organisations producing practical and useful information about bullying. These include:

Anti-bullying Alliance
www.nch.org/aba 020 7843 6000

Anti-bullying Campaign
020 7378 1446

Anti-bullying Guidance for Schools
Safe to Learn: Embedding Anti-bullying Work in Schools (DCSF 2007)
The anti-bullying Guidance for Schools guide to recognising, preventing and dealing with bullying. Department of Health and the DCSF in partnership with the Children's Commissioner and the Anti-bullying Alliance

Are You Talking to Me?
Young people's participation in anti-bullying, an Anti-bullying Alliance resource (2006).

Bullying UK
www.bullying.co.uk

Childline
www.childline.org.uk 020 7239 1000

'Cyber-bullying on the rise among primary pupils', *TES*, 21 March 2008, Jonathan Milne.

Cyberbullying: Safe to Learn: Embedding Anti-bullying Work in Schools (DCSF 2007). www.teachernet.gov.uk

DCSF (2007) *Guidance for Safer Working Practice for Adults who Work with Children and Young People.*

DCSF (2007) *The Use of Force to Control or Restrain Pupils: Non-statutory Guidance for Schools in England.*

DCSF (2008) *The Children's Plan Progress Report.*

Elliot, Michelle (1994) *Keeping Safe: A Practical Guide to Talking to Children.* London: Coronet Books.

Healthy Schools
www.healthyschools.org.uk

Kidscape
Bullying advice, helpline, information, anti-bullying resources and training
020 7730 3300
www.kidscape.org.uk

Safe to Learn: Embedding Anti-bullying Work in Schools Overview (DCSF).
www.teachernet.gov.uk

SEAL
http://nationalstrategies.standards.dcsf.gov.uk/primary/publications/banda/seal/

Smith, Peter (2000) *Bullying: Don't Suffer in Silence: An Anti-Bullying Pack for Schools.*
www.dfes.gov.uk/bullying

Thomas Coram Research Unit (2003) *Tackling Bullying: Listening to the Views of Children and Young People.* London: DfES.

Healthy eating

Introduction

Eating food is generally a very pleasurable experience which meets a range of our physical, social and emotional needs. Up to 30 per cent of a child's daily food is eaten during school hours and a school lunch should provide a growing child with one third of the recommended daily nutritional intake. Research undertaken by the Institute of Education has found that children who have a nutritious diet 'are five times as likely to behave well, pay attention and work harder than those whose meals were less nutritious' (*TES*, 22 August 2008). There is an obesity crisis in the UK, with more than a quarter of schoolchildren overweight or obese. On current trends nearly 60 per cent of the British population would be obese by 2050 (Foresight report on obesity, *The Lancet*). In response to such concerns, the government and schools are working in a determined way to counteract pressures from advertising and to change children's lifestyles and attitudes to food and exercise.

LTSs are front-line players in helping children to eat healthily. They are the people in the dining room who are responsible for ensuring that in a relatively short time, large numbers of children are well behaved, safe, happy and eating a well balanced meal.

What should we eat?

The huge amount of information about healthy eating can be overwhelming and it is so easy to switch off and ignore guidance. It is, however, crucial to know what constitutes a balanced diet so that you can remain healthy and help to educate the children you work with.

Eight tips for eating well

1 Base your meals on starchy food – carbohydrates – which is a good source of energy and fibre, calcium, iron and vitamin B.

2 Eat lots of fruit and vegetables – try to eat at least five portions per day (fresh, frozen or tinned). This can help to prevent heart disease and some cancers. All four- to six-year-old children in infant and special schools are entitled to a free piece of fruit or vegetable each school day.

3 Eat more fish – two portions per week including one portion of oily fish, which is an excellent source of omega 3. This appears to reduce your risk of heart disease, lowers blood pressure, reduces blood clotting, enhances immune function and improves arthritis symptoms.

4 Cut down on saturated fat and sugar. Too much saturated fat increases cholesterol in the blood which can lead to heart disease. Unsaturated fat, found in vegetable oil, nuts and seeds, reduce cholesterol. Most people in the UK eat too much sugar which is high in calories and rots teeth.

5 Eat less salt – no more than six grams a day for anyone over 11 years old, and less for younger children. The majority of people eat too much salt, much of which is already in food. Too much salt raises blood pressure which can lead to heart disease.

6 Get active and try to achieve a healthy weight. Physical activity uses up extra calories. If we eat more than our body needs we put on weight because unused energy is stored as fat.

7 Drink plenty of water – six to eight glasses of water or other fluids per day stops dehydration.

8 Don't skip breakfast – it can provide energy as well as essential nutrients. There is some evidence to suggest that eating breakfast can help people control their weight (Food Standards Agency, *Eat Well – Be Well* (http://www.eatwell.gov.uk/healthydiet/eighttipssection/8tips/)).

The Food Standards Agency, an independent watchdog states: 'The two keys to a healthy diet are eating the right amount of food for how active you are, and eating a range of foods to make sure you are getting a balanced diet'. They recommend 'The eatwell plate', another useful guide aimed at helping to achieve a balanced diet.

The eatwell plate
© Crown copyright material is reproduced with the permission of the Controller of HMSO and Queen's Printer for Scotland.

It outlines five groups of food and shows the percentage of our daily intake that each group should be. The groups are:

1 carbohydrates (bread, rice, pasta, potatoes)
2 fruit and vegetables
3 protein (meat, fish, eggs, beans)
4 dairy (milk, yoghurt, butter, cheese)
5 food high in sugar and fat.

Approximately one third of food eaten should be carbohydrates, one third should be fruit and vegetables and the final third should be comprised of the three remaining categories. Food and drink high in sugar and fat should make up the smallest category.

The new food-based and nutrient-based standards for school meals

A nutrient is food or chemicals that we need to live and grow or a substance used in an organism's metabolism, which must be taken in from its environment. Until fairly recently, the food served in schools was low in nutrients and often of a generally poor standard. It contained too much starchy food cooked in oil or fat, high quantities of sugar and salt and inadequate amounts of fruit, fibre, calcium, iron and vitamins.

Since 2005, as the result of the impressive initiatives started by Jamie Oliver, the quality of food provided by school has greatly improved. Following a huge petition, the government pledged millions of pounds to this cause. The School Food Trust is an independent organisation which was established by the government in September 2005 to help move things forward (www.schoolfoodtrust.org.uk).

In September 2006, the New Interim Food Based Lunch Standards were introduced which banned junk food and ensured schools provide: high-quality meat, poultry or oily fish and at least two portions of fruit and vegetables with every meal, plus bread, cereals and potatoes regularly. Schools are required to regulate the amounts of 14 specific nutrients, including saturated fat, salt, iron and vitamins, in individual school dinners. Free fresh drinking water must be available at all times.

The standards state that deep-fried food must be limited to no more than two portions per week. Fizzy drinks, biscuits, crisps, chocolate and other confectioneries are removed from school meals and vending machines. Condiments such as ketchup and mayonnaise should only be available in sachets and manufactured meat products such as burgers and chicken nuggets may be served occasionally, but only if they meet standards for minimum meat content.

For more information visit www.schoolfoodtrust.org.uk and click on 'Guide to the nutrient-based standards'.

Guidelines for drinks in school

In 2007 the School Food Trust created a voluntary code of practice for drinks provided in schools. Drinks should have no added artificial sweeteners, colours or added natural sweeteners (except milk drinks to encourage the consumption of a key source of calcium). There should be no other additives except those necessary for stability, regulation of acidity and the preservation of fruit juices. Fortification should be used only where there is evidence of a clear and focused public health benefit.

ACTIVITY 1

Discuss the following. Is it true that:

1 Schools cannot serve cheese?
2 Schools cannot use salt in cooking?
3 Schools cannot serve cakes and biscuits?
4 Schools cannot put butter on jacket potatoes?
5 Schools cannot serve chips?
6 Schools cannot provide jam or honey to spread on bread or toast?
7 Schools cannot dilute fruit juice with water?
8 Schools cannot serve bacon at breakfast?
9 The standards are only guidelines and are not law?

Here are the answers:

1 Schools can serve cheese at any time of the school day. It is good practice to use low fat varieties of cheese.

2 Salt is permitted in the cooking process but should not be provided at lunch tables or at service counters. It is good practice to reduce the amount of salt used in cooking, adding herbs and spices to flavour dishes instead.

3 Cakes and biscuits can be served at lunchtimes as long as they contain no confectionery (chocolate and chocolate products, sweets and chewy bars). Children should only be encouraged to eat these as part of a meal following, but not instead of, a main course.

4 Butter is permitted on jacket potatoes. This does not count as a starchy food cooked in fat or oil as the butter is added after the cooking process. It is good practice to restrict the amount of butter added to a jacket potato.

5 Deep-fried foods (e.g. chips) can be served up to twice a week across the school day.

6 Jam and honey are not restricted by the standards. It is good practice to limit servings of jam and honey because they are high in sugar.

7 Fruit juice can be diluted with water provided that the fruit juice component in the final drink is at least 50 per cent by volume.

8 Bacon is not restricted by the standards. It is good practice to grill rather than fry bacon and to vary the types of foods served at breakfast.

9 Schools are required to meet the standards by law.

(From the Food Trust website: 'Food-based myths')

Healthy schools

More than 97 per cent of schools nationally are now involved in the Healthy Schools programme and over 70 per cent have achieved National Healthy School status. To obtain Healthy School status, schools are required to have a named member of the senior leadership team (SLT) to oversee all aspects of food in schools and a whole school food policy which invoves children and their parents. There are 11 compulsory criteria to meet. For further information visit www.healthyschools.gov.uk

Initiatives to encourage healthy eating and the uptake of school dinners

Changing attitudes is a slow process. Initially, following the revolution in school meals, there was a decrease in the uptake of healthier cooked food and a move towards children opting for often less nutritious packed lunches. The government has made considerable efforts to improve this trend and statistics show gradual progress. In many schools children, parents and carers are provided with regular information about the benefits of school dinners. Menus are sent home and parents are also invited to school to taste food and help with cookery clubs. There is some concern that the increased cost of healthy ingredients is making school meals too expensive, particularly in times of recession. In Scotland and some areas of England and Wales, free school meals have been provided to all children in an attempt to improve the nation's poor diet and health.This is likely to be extended in the future. From September 2009, Ofsted inspections will be monitoring school lunch uptake.

Packed lunch initiatives

Approximately 50 per cent of primary school children bring a packed lunch to school on a daily basis. A survey by the Food Standards Agency showed that a high proportion of these contained white bread sandwiches, crisps and a biscuit or a chocolate bar. Many schools have produced guidelines, information and sample menus for healthier packed lunches and some have introduced classes for parents to learn to provide healthier options. There are useful links on the School Food Trust website under 'Packed Lunch Links' (http://www.schoolfoodtrust.org.uk/).

Eating lunch is a sociable time at which pupils often care more about being with friends than about the food they eat. Children having packed lunches and school dinners are found to benefit from being allowed to sit together. Children may opt into having school dinners, having tried out their friends' food. Schools often allow less healthy options to be included in lunch boxes once a week as children having school dinners are allowed cakes for pudding as part of the cooked meal.

The role of the LTS – helping children to eat a healthy lunch

For real change to take place in children's food intake and attitude, the whole school community needs to be involved. Schools are likely to have a whole school food policy which outlines expectations about food including school dinners and packed lunches. LTSs need to be aware of the school's expectations and what to do if the rules are breached. It also helps to discuss ideas and initiatives with others, and many schools are setting up School Food Groups which include LTSs, catering staff, governors, teaching staff, parents and children. If this is not happening in your school, discuss the possibility with your line manager.

As LTSs, you play a vital role in helping to create the right atmosphere and guiding children to eat healthily. You can be effective by:

- Creating a comfortable, friendly environment in the dining room
- Helping children to develop socially at lunchtime
- Encouraging children to choose and eat healthy food
- Coping with faddy eaters
- Monitoring what children are eating
- Consulting children about their preferences
- Keeping an eye open for children who may be experiencing problems in relation to food
- Offering children some educational input about healthy eating.

Creating a comfortable, friendly environment in the dining room

The atmosphere in the school dining room will have a direct effect on children's happiness and eating choices. Historically, dining rooms have been noisy and chaotic, but schools are putting money and energy into improvements. An attractive, well planned environment, where pupils feel a degree of ownership, improves behaviour and social interaction during mealtimes. In June 2007 the government issued *A Fresh Look at the School Meal Experience,* which covers a wide range of recommendations and case studies. The guidelines explore how best to organise the dining space, seat and involve children, reduce noise, manage lunchtime queues, promote healthy options and improve relationships between staff and pupils. Details can be found on the School Food Trust website (http://www.schoolfoodtrust.org.uk/).

Helping children to develop socially at lunchtime

In recent years family habits have changed and the regular coming together to share food is often replaced by takeaway meals and snacking in front of the television. Children starting school may need to be taught the basics, including how to sit at a table to eat, and to use a knife and fork. As stated in earlier chapters, you have a clear role in helping children to develop social skills at this important part of the day.

CASE STUDY 1

In one school the staff introduced a system where children of mixed ages ate lunch together on brightly decorated tables. If possible, a teacher, teaching assistant or buddy would join them for part of the meal. Background music was played and some group discussions were encouraged. This had a positive impact on all age groups.

ACTIVITY 2

Complete the dining room checklist below.

In your school...	Yes	No
Is the dining room well decorated and attractive?	☐	☐
Are pictures in the dining room culturally sensitive?	☐	☐
Is the furniture suitable?	☐	☐
Are the children rushed when eating?	☐	☐
Is there sufficient space to sit comfortably?	☐	☐
Would you like to eat in this environment?	☐	☐
Is the noise level in the dining room acceptable?	☐	☐
Do you have systems to gain children's attention and reduce the noise without having to resort to shouting?	☐	☐
Do you discuss seating arrangements and other practicalities with the children?	☐	☐
Are the dining room rules and routines clear and on display?	☐	☐
Are children required to wait in queues for an unacceptable amount of time?	☐	☐
Do you consult with children about the dining room atmosphere?	☐	☐
Do you think about improvements on a regular basis?	☐	☐

If any of the answers are 'No', what can be changed?

Although the responsibility for making major changes rests with senior managers and governors, you are required to consult children, feed back concerns and suggest improvements.

Encouraging children to eat healthy options

Children have the right to make choices about what they eat, and too much pressure can cause long-term problems. Their likes and appetites will vary greatly and unlike many adults, the majority of children eat when they are hungry rather than bored or unhappy. It is the adults in their life who tend to worry about their food intake, and children are quick to pick up on this anxiety. It helps to remain calm and to try not to nag or fight over food. Never attempt to force a child to eat as this can result in an unhelpful power struggle. Encouraging children to make healthy choices, though, is a fundamental part of your job and proactive LTSs encourage children to eat adequate amounts of a variety of healthy food. Although you may not be directly involved at the serving stage, you can be influential when children are choosing or have sat down with their food.

Cultural influences

Food preferences may also vary depending on the child's cultural background. It is helpful to have some understanding of this, and children are often happy to discuss their family traditions in relation to food. Schools are likely to provide food to reflect their population's taste. LTSs have a particular role in encouraging children to accept, understand and respect the food of others.

Parental pressures

Parents may have strong opinions about what and how much their children eat, and LTSs describe how they can be 'caught in the middle' of conflicting opinions. For example, some parents want their child to finish everything on their plate or in their lunchbox. Others prefer their children to choose what and how much they eat. LTSs can feel pressurised by catering staff or senior managers who have firm opinions about similar issues. On occasions children may refuse to eat the food their parents have given them. This is not easy, but clear and honest communication with relevant people can help.

Reward systems

Schools use a range of schemes to reward healthy eating. These include offering verbal praise, stickers or house points and certificates. Details of resource providers have been included at the end of this chapter.

CASE STUDY 2

LTSs in a London school were concerned by how many children were walking past the salad bar without considering these options. They agreed to take turns to stand near the salad bar and to encourage children to try the food. The uptake of salad improved.

One primary school developed a system of stickers and a Healthy Eater of the Week certificate to be awarded in assembly for the child who has the healthiest lunchbox. The lunchtime supervisors selected pupils for these awards.

Another school noticed that at lunchtime the fruit bowl which contained cut-up fruit was hidden behind less healthy options. Following discussion with the catering staff they agreed to put cut-up fruit on each table. Children who regularly eat fruit or salad were rewarded with a healthy eating sticker.

Coping with faddy eaters

Research suggests that many babies reject new tastes and textures and it can take 10–14 tastes before a food will be accepted ('Too much, too young', *The Guardian*, 29 January 2007), so don't be put off by children's negative responses. A training package devised by Sunderland Council entitled 'Let's Make Lunchtime Fun' outlines how, when young children see a wide range of foods regularly, they start to accept them more readily, especially if they see other children enjoying them. If children are unhappy about trying new foods they suggest lunchtime staff and parents adopt the attitude, 'You don't like it today but you might like it another day'. They also suggest talking to children about how our tastes change as we grow and encouraging them to see liking new foods as a normal part of growing up. For more information visit http://www.schoolfoodtrust.org.uk/search_detail.asp?PId=263&searchterm=lets%20make%20lunchtime%20fun%20sunderland%20council

Monitor children's lunches

LTSs have an important monitoring role. You can oversee children's choices, how much is eaten and what type of food children have in their lunchboxes. LTSs have described a range of inappropriate food found in children's lunchboxes.

> **CASE STUDY 3**
>
> In one school, an LTS became aware that a girl was bringing only doughnuts to school every day. In another school cold chips wrapped in newspaper were often in a boy's lunchbox.

You are required to report concerns and to have a full discussion with your managers about what to do if children bring packed lunchboxes containing banned food.

> **CASE STUDY 4**
>
> An LTS decided to confiscate items from children's lunchboxes that she believed to be unsuitable. A number of parents, understandably, became angry and complained. The head teacher took action by providing parents and children with information about healthy eating and included them in full discussions about acceptable options.

Consult children about their food preferences and opinions

You are in an excellent position to talk to children about their preferences and to feedback the responses to the relevant people. You will know how the children feel about options on offer and how their tastes develop. Interestingly, from surveying children, we learn that children prefer different types of food to be served separately, and so are more likely to enjoy salad if the ingredients are not mixed together. You will also be aware of how effective dining room initiatives and organisational changes have been. With the help of your managers you can also offer pupils more formal questionnaires or discussion groups.

> **CASE STUDY 5**
>
> LTSs were concerned that the vegetarian children were being offered an extremely poor choice every day. They were also concerned that the portions of food being offered were insufficient. They reported this to their line manager regularly.

CASE STUDY 6

A proactive LTS noticed that children were throwing away large amounts of pasta or rice with sauce. She discovered that far more was being eaten when the pasta and sauce were separated on the children's plates. Changes were made, for the better.

CASE STUDY 7

LTSs were concerned by the treatment of the children by the serving staff. The head teacher arranged a meeting with the LTS and the servers to attempt to agree on acceptable practice. The senior LTS attended school council meetings on a half-termly basis to discuss lunchtime organisation and food issues. The children requested specific food options and types of seating arrangements. It was also agreed that music would be played in the dining room as long as the noise level did not rise to unacceptable levels.

ACTIVITY 3

Complete the food checklist

	Yes	No
Are you aware of a whole school food policy?	☐	☐
How do you promote and encourage healthy eating at your school?	☐	☐
What systems do you have to reward healthy eating?	☐	☐
Are your school dinners of a good quality?	☐	☐
Is the food presented in an attractive way?	☐	☐
How do you cope with faddy or reluctant eaters?	☐	☐
Are children offered adequate choices and portion sizes?	☐	☐
Are children's cultural and dietary needs catered for?	☐	☐
Does your school have guidelines or a policy about packed lunches?	☐	☐
Do you know what you are expected to do if children bring in food that is banned?	☐	☐
Do you know what to do if you are concerned that a child is regularly not eating enough lunch?	☐	☐
Do children eating packed lunches and school dinners sit together?	☐	☐
Do you consult with children on a regular basis about food preferences?	☐	☐
Do you inform relevant people about children's preferences?	☐	☐

Keep an eye out for problems children may be experiencing in relation to food

As well as healthy bodies, we want children to have a healthy relationship with their food. Infants will start school with extremely different experiences of eating, which experts believe can shape their future attitudes. Observant LTSs are likely to become aware of the children who are developing eating difficulties. Some children are naturally cautious about trying new things. Others have a strong dislike of certain textures or smells.

Children start to worry about their body size at an increasingly early age and it is not unusual for young KS1 girls to talk about dieting. Discussion about food intake needs to be handled sensitively. The scale of eating disorders in very young children is rising significantly in both boys and girls and can start as early as six years old (Haines and Neumark-Sztainer 2006). For overweight children it is best not to talk about their weight; it is more helpful to focus more generally on healthy eating and exercise.

Many young people experience difficulties with eating food at some time in their lives. These can range from not liking foods (which happens to most people from time to time) or experiencing a trauma in life which in turn may effect you emotionally, leading to clinical eating disorders such as anorexia nervosa, bulimia, or compulsive eating . . . Many people who have eating problems feel bad about themselves or are living in stressful family situations. The eating problem is often a mask for other issues or could be a way of trying to cope with them . . . Any number of other issues can 'trigger' an eating problem. It may come from a mixture of problems, such as pressure to be thin, bullying, abuse, the death of someone close.

ChildLine (www.childline.org.uk/Info/DamagingYourself/Pages/EatingProblems.aspx)

 If you have concerns about a child's eating or attitude to food, pass this on to a teacher or senior manager. Serious concern should be treated in the same way as child protection issues as a child's wellbeing may be at risk.

Offer children some educational input about healthy eating

Many healthy eating initiatives are found to work in the short term but prove difficult to sustain. Research by the Food Trust suggests we still have a long way to go. Primary school children have poor knowledge of fruit and vegetables and are not eating enough of them. Children are aware of the term 'healthy eating', but confuse it with a low-calorie diet. For further information visit http://www.schoolfoodtrust.org.uk/content.asp?ContentId=381

You do not need to be a nutritional expert to offer simple information about how certain foods can help growth, health and development. You can do this in the dining room, the playground and classroom during wet play. It helps if discussions and activities are enjoyable. These may include:

- Games like food bingo, word games and memory games
- Topics for table discussion, for example, 'What meal would you cook if you had your favourite celebrity coming for tea?'
- Queue activities, for example, 'Foody Chinese whispers'
- Practical activities like food tasting sessions
- Design activities, e.g. create a menu theme day. Design a food collage or a healthy eating poster.

Sunderland Council's 'Lets Make Lunchtime Fun' resource pack includes a range of activity sheets and games which you can obtain on the Food Trust website. There are also sheets and activities for younger children on the Kizclub website (www.kizclub.com). 'Eat well – be well' provides interactive games for children. These can be used during wet play if children have access to computers (www.eatwell.gov.uk). You can use your imagination and adapt existing games, or create new food quizzes.

Other initiatives that LTSs can become involved with

- Join a Healthy Eating Working Party in your school
- Create ways to reward children for healthy eating

- Use wet play to provide activities and to encourage children to talk about healthy eating issues
- Involve the children you work with; ask their opinion about food and dining room initiatives
- Encourage older children, monitors or buddies to help children with healthy choices
- Help with existing school initiatives including cooking classes, gardening clubs or school trips to farms.

CASE STUDY 8

In one school the senior LTS, a keen gardener, ran a club for children who wanted to grow vegetables. As well as having great fun, she was able to use the time to discuss the value of the food grown. She also initiated tasting sessions and games, including food bingo, during wet play.

A simple healthy eating quiz was given to KS2 children during wet play, with a prize for the winner. KS1 children were asked to design healthy eating posters for the dining room.

Training

Many lunchtime supervisors are now being offered training in healthy eating issues. This may be provided by your education authority or by your school. There are courses available that lead to accredited qualifications. These include accredited Level 1 in Nutrition and in 'Providing a Healthier School Meals Service'. There are also Level 2 and 3 qualifications available, and The Support Work in Schools award includes relevant units in this area. To find out more you can visit the School Trust website (www.schoolfoodtrust.org.uk) and search for training and qualifications or discuss options with your line manager.

Every Child Matters and healthy eating

The table below looks at the lunchtime supervisor's role in supporting the five *ECM* outcomes in relation to healthy eating in school.

ECM outcomes	The lunchtime supervisor's role in supporting the five *ECM* outcomes in relation to healthy eating in school
Be healthy	Be aware of your whole school food policy
	Encourage children to make healthy choices in relation to their food and drink intake
	Monitor food eaten to ensure a balanced diet
	Encourage children to try new foods and to develop a positive relationship to eating/drinking
	Support and encourage faddy eaters
	Help children develop a range of social and emotional learning through a positive dining room experience
	Help children to understand the link between food intake and health
	Encourage children to be tolerant towards food from a range of cultures

Stay safe	Set clear and safe rules and expectations for behaviour in the dining room
	Have high expectations and plan for positive behaviour and co-operation
	Organise the dining room to ensure maximum safety
	Ensure that children with eating difficulties are monitored and supported
Enjoy and achieve	Provide a happy, enjoyable eating experience for children
	Regularly review the dining room environment
	Ensure that the children can choose and enjoy their food and drink
	Provide clear praise and rewards for positive healthy choices and positive behaviour
	Monitor children's preferences and report these back to the providers
	Encourage inclusion and independence for all pupils
Make a positive contribution	Ensure pupils are consulted regularly and offer feedback about food options and dining room initiatives
	Encourage children to be assertive about what they would like to eat and drink
	Encourage children to understand and to take responsibility for their health and food intake
	Encourage monitors/buddies and other children to support each other in the dining room
Achieve economic wellbeing	Encourage children to contribute to dining room organisation
	Encourage leadership, independence and teamwork
	Empower children to initiate and develop activities.

Conclusion

Eating is usually a pleasurable activity which directly affects our physical health and emotional wellbeing. There is a great deal you can do to encourage children to eat healthily and to develop a positive attitude to food. The information and ideas outlined in this chapter can help you to make a real difference.

Useful organisations and resources

British Nutrition Foundation (www.nutrition.org.uk)
This site provides healthy eating information and resources for schools.

Childline
(www.childline.org.uk/Info/DamagingYourself/Pages/EatingProblems.aspx)

Comic Company (www.comiccompany.co.uk)
Provides lunchbox stickers.

Eat Well – Be Well
A website for children with interactive games (www.eatwell.gov.uk).

The Eatwell Plate
Food Standards Agency (www.food.gov.uk).

Food – A Fact of Life (www.foodafactoflife.org.uk)
Provides a progressive approach to teaching about healthy eating, cooking, food and farming from 3 to 16 years.

Food for Life (www.foodforlife.org.uk)
Offers resources and information on how schools and communities across England can transform food culture.

Food in Schools
A training programme to enhance knowledge, skills and understanding about food and cooking.

Food Standards Agency (www.food.gov.uk)
An Independent watchdog established to protect the public's health and consumer interests in relation to food safety.

Foresight report on obesity (K. McPherson, T. Marsh and M. Brown)
The Lancet, 370, (9601), 1755.

A Fresh Look at the School Meal Experience (DCSF 2007)

'Good food can cause mischief'
Adi Bloom, *Times Educational Supplement*, 22 August 2008.

Haines, J. and Neumark-Sztainer, D. (2006) 'Prevention of obesity and eating disorders: a consideration of shared risk factors' *Health Education Research* 21(6), 770–82.

Healthy Lives, Brighter Futures: The Strategy for Children and Young People's Health, February 2009.

Healthy Lunchbox (www.healthylunchbox.co.uk)
Advice on creating a healthy lunchbox for children

Healthy Schools (www.healthyschools.gov.uk)

Kizclub (www.kizclub.com/Topics/food)
Wet play activities.

School Food Trust (www.schoolfoodtrust.org.uk)
An organisation to improve the nutrition of school meals, providing news, information, guidance, resources and research.

Let's Make Lunchtimes Fun
Sunderland Council resource pack on the School Food Trust website (www.schoolfoodtrust.org.uk/UploadDocs/contents/Documents/resources_pack.pdf).

Packed lunches
There are useful links on the School Food Trust website under *Packed Lunch* links. www.schoolfoodtrust.org.uk

Sustain Web (www.sustainweb)
The Children's Food Campaign.

The School FEAST Network (www.schoolfeast.co.uk)
Provides training and support for all school meal providers and staff.

'Too much, too young'
Lucy Atkins, *The Guardian*, Monday, 29 January 2007.

Play at lunchtime

Introduction

When children are happily occupied at lunchtime, schools describe how behaviour improves dramatically. This chapter will explore how and why children play, and the important opportunity for play and physical activity offered by the lunchtime break. It will go on to examine playground organisation and a range of options that can be offered to pupils at lunchtime.

Until recently the lunchtime break was viewed mainly as a time for everyone to eat, for children and teachers to have a welcome rest from each other and for children to let off steam to aid their afternoon concentration. Schools now recognise that, when well managed, the lunchtime session can also contribute to children's wellbeing, development, learning and behaviour.

Physical activity

Due to changes in lifestyle, children are often at home in front of the television or the computer screen. Many lack exercise and we are facing an obesity crisis. In response, the government is focusing on children's eating and activity levels. The DCSF's *PE and Sports*

Strategy 2008 outlines how many schools are now providing at least two hours' high-quality PE and sports to children aged 5 to 16. There is now an expectation, that schools in partnership with other sport providers will strive to increase this amount of sporting activity from two to five hours per week (*Healthy Lives, Brighter Futures: The Strategy for Children and Young People's Health,* February 2009).

The importance of the lunchtime break

The school playground provides a major opportunity for children to be physically active and to play freely in an outdoor space. The government Play Strategy (2008) acknowledges the importance of both structured and unstructured play for children's physical and emotional wellbeing.

Play England, a lottery funded organisation specialising in all aspects of children's play. writes:

> The school day should allow time for children to relax and play freely with friends. Young children learn best through play and, as they get older, play supports and enriches their learning…in school, time and space for play and outdoor leaning is as important as formal teaching. School grounds should be good places to play.
>
> (Play England 2007)

Blatchford (1998) discusses how, at lunchtime, children benefit greatly from periods of relative freedom from adult control when they can pursue friendships and create their own social worlds. He warns against the trend to shorten lunchtime and playtime, believing that children's emotional wellbeing will suffer.

What is play and why do children need it?

Children and adults benefit from playing. To play is one of the rights of the child under the United Nations Convention, and if denied the opportunity, children are likely to suffer. Play is active, often spontaneous and can be done alone or with others. It is also a process which involves doing, exploring and testing out different types of behaviour. Play enables children to develop physically, socially, emotionally and intellectually. Through play children develop necessary social skills including how to co-operate, negotiate, take turns and abide by rules.

Play can be therapeutic and helps children to cope with their powerful emotions. Children facing distress or trauma are likely to act it out in their play in an attempt to make sense of painful events.

The way children play

Children can play in many different ways depending on their physical needs and their personality. Their play will also influenced by their age, their stage of development and their gender. For example, very young children find it difficult to play with others without considerable adult input. As children get older they are more able to cope with complex rules and structures in games.

Gender differences

In the playground boys tend to play in larger groups and are more physical. They are also more likely to argue about rules and leadership. Girls are more likely to play or talk in pairs or smaller groups, and are likely to be less aggressive (White and Wilkinson 2000). LTSs describe how girls' disputes can be complex and drawn out, often lasting for weeks and involving large numbers of children.

Types of play

Children need the opportunity for free unstructured play in which they can be themselves, make their own decisions and play in their own way. They also benefit when adults structure the play. Research suggests that, mainly for safety reasons, adults are at risk of over-controlling children's activities in the playground. Maintaining health and safety in the playground is a major priority and LTSs tread a fine line between keeping children as safe as possible and allowing them to play in a free, exciting and challenging way. This will be explored further in Chapter 10.

According to White and Wilkinson, the majority of children's play involves physical contact, particularly in the case of younger children where rough and tumble and chasing make up a significant proportion of their games. The benefits and difficulties associated with such behaviour have been discussed in Chapter 6, page 61.

Creating a positive playground ethos

LTSs are key players in creating a positive playground ethos. Playgrounds have been found to become happier places when:

- LTSs are offered training to enable them to interact and play with children
- Children are offered appropriate play materials and types of playground activities
- Playgrounds are zoned and offer a variety of activities.

Interacting and playing with children

There will be times when children are happily playing and need little adult intervention. On other occasions they may need your assistance. You are likely to make a considerable difference to the quality of lunchtime by introducing and teaching games. One enthusiastic LTS described how 'lunchtime feels like my playtime too'.

When LTSs are actively and constructively involved in play, they are on hand to de-escalate conflict, channel play fighting into organised activities, act as positive role models for children who are struggling to sort out arguments and to support isolated children. You can join in with children's play in a number of ways, ranging from turning a rope to teaching a new game. You can also make suggestions and initiate play when necessary, whilst allowing the children to make their own decisions whenever possible. How much you join in and stay in the game will depend on children's needs and the demands on your time.

Teaching games

ACTIVITY 1

Can you remember the games you played in the playground when you were a child?

Would you be able to teach any of these to the children at school?

How could this be organised?

There has recently been an interest in re-teaching traditional playground games which you may wish to find out more about by contacting your local education authority and asking for the PE and school sport co-ordinator. Teaching children games can be demanding and will need to be carefully paced. The game should be played often enough to familiarise the children, without becoming over-familiar and boring.

When teaching games it is important to give simple and clear instructions. You may also need to demonstrate how to play, and to repeat the instructions a number of times to ensure that children understand. This skill can be developed with practice, and it may help to observe others teaching games.

advice

CASE STUDY 1

A LTS described repeating a simple playground game for 15 minutes every day for a week, to familiarise the children. She then had a break, and returned to the game two weeks later. The children welcomed its return and remembered the rules well enough to join in quickly.

Can you play and supervise the playground at the same time?

Some LTSs will honestly say that they do not particularly want to play with the children although they are happy to offer support and help to pick up the pieces when things go wrong. Others describe the pressures of keeping children safe at the same time as attempting to play. One enthusiastic LTS described her experience in a busy infant school:

> I just get a game of skipping going, and am turning the rope, when a child behind me has an accident or a group of children start to fight. By the time I have sorted things out, the skipping activity that was going so well has collapsed and the children are arguing.

Schools may overcome this by employing play leaders with special responsibilities for play. Others recruit specific members of the LTS team to lead the play, whilst others focus on supervising the playground. This requires an adequately staffed team, flexible practice and excellent organisation.

ACTIVITY 2

In your school how do you manage the conflicting demands of playing whilst supervising the playground?

How could things be improved?

Providing appropriate play equipment and playground activities

The size of the playground will affect the type of equipment and the range of activities that you can offer. Even the smallest of playgrounds can be managed imaginatively and children have an impressive ability to adapt to fit the existing space. The range of equipment used by schools is extensive and a list of providers is included at the end of this chapter.

Maintaining and replacing equipment

Staff often complain that children lack respect for the equipment and that most of it ends up in pieces or on the roof. Children need to share responsibility for their equipment and it also helps to lock it in a safe place, preferably separate from the PE cupboard. No matter how hard you try, playground equipment will need replacing. Schools often fundraise to purchase and replace it.

ACTIVITY 3

Do you have enough playground equipment?

Is it varied and interesting?

Do you have a locked area to store it in?

Who maintains and checks the equipment in your school?

Could this happen more systematically?

Organised sport

Schools with adequate space and staff numbers may offer children the chance to participate in organised sports at lunchtime. Play leaders or delegated LTSs may have special responsibility for overseeing the activities, often organised on a rota basis in a particular area of the playground.

Competitive games and co-operative games

Children play co-operatively when they help each other to achieve an agreed goal and where there are no winners or losers. Examples are skipping, dance or circle games. Competitive games, such as football or netball, have winners and losers. Children find it difficult to lose at any age, and for younger ones this can be particularly distressing. It is an important lesson to learn and when dealt with sensitively, children can develop through the experience. Competition can act to motivate and challenge and you will need to achieve a balance between healthy competition and co-operative play.

Guidelines for keeping lunchtime activities successful

Decide:

- Where the equipment will be stored; you will need a locked space
- Which games will be played each week. Consider playing one or two games on a daily basis for at least a week before introducing a new one
- What time and for how long will the activity take place. It may only be 15 minutes per lunchtime
- Who will be responsible for drawing up a rota for the children's participation and LTS's involvement
- Who will be responsible for collecting and returning the equipment
- Who will decide when and how the buddies are to be involved
- How will you target reluctant children.

Things to do:

- Check the equipment on a regular basis
- Promote the activities in a whole school assembly
- Discuss expectations with other staff and the buddies
- Ensure everyone is clear about the practicalities
- Encourage children who are reluctant to join in
- Review and plan the activities at regular intervals
- Adapt the activities to meet the needs of your children.

Fixed play equipment and playground markings

Fixed playground equipment can provide children with stimulation, adventure, comfort and privacy. It needs to be carefully selected and maintained. Appropriate floor covering will also be necessary to reduce the risk of injury. A study by Liverpool University showed that activity levels of five- to seven-year-olds increased by 20 per cent once playground markings had been added. Although commercial firms provide floor or wall markings for playgrounds, the most successful have been found to be those that have involved and consulted the children for ideas.

Zoning and enclosing areas of the playground for specific activities

A survey of 700 schools in England showed that those which had transformed their grounds by zoning, reported a 64 per cent reduction in bullying and a 28 per cent decrease in vandalism. Children's attitudes to learning improved significantly and they played better together.

(Northern 2004)

Many schools decide to create active and quiet areas in the playground, this requires consultation and careful planning.

Inclusive play

When developing activities, you are required to plan to meet the needs of a wide range of pupils attending school. This may include boys and girls, able and disabled pupils, children with special needs, younger and less boisterous children. The Youth Sport Trust and Sainsbury's Active Kids have created TOP Activity, a programme of 'alternative' sport and physical activities designed for use in a range of settings including primary school playgrounds. It aims to engage 'hard to reach' children aged 7–11 years-old not currently participating in more traditional sports. For more information visit www.youthsporttrust.org/page/topactivity/index.html

ACTIVITY 4

Which groups of children do you think have the worst time in your playground?

How could this be improved?

How do you provide for the less boisterous and non-sporty children?

How do you ensure that the disabled or special need pupils are included?

Does your playground interest the girls as much as the boys?

Below are some examples of practice developed by schools to include a wide range of pupils.

CASE STUDY 2

In one playground boys playing football dominated the majority of the space. The girls become marginalised and excluded. In response to this, a meeting was called to discuss the problem with the children. It was agreed that football was to be restricted to a smaller area and girls were offered female-only football once a week.

CASE STUDY 3

At a school which accommodated able-bodied and physically disabled children, a separate soft-surface area was created in the playground so that children could play on the floor without being trampled on by those participating in more boisterous activities. Both disabled and able-bodied children used this resource.

CASE STUDY 4

One school created a special quiet playground zone for children who wanted to participate in 'calm activities'. A supervisor ensured that board games, drawing materials, books and construction toys were provided, and that children who wished to play more boisterously were directed to a different area.

Play with younger children

The playground can be a scary place for small children, who are likely to need support, nurturing and encouragement. Young children benefit from the security of developing close relationships with familiar supervisors. Very small children may lack language or verbal communication skills, especially if English is not their first language or if they have special educational needs. You will need to check that the child has understood your communication, and be prepared to rephrase or act it out when necessary. When supervising small children who are playing freely, it may help to observe the game and to join in only when invited, or when you think it necessary. If possible, be led by the children and attempt to enter into their world, rather than trying to control the play. You can do this by watching carefully and by asking the occasional question. Children are often happy to explain their play and to tell you what they would like you to do.

CASE STUDY 5

One LTS described how a small group of children invited her to hop over the leaves in the playground, which led to the princess's palace. She enjoyed joining in with the children's elaborate fantasy, and described how on one occasion she sought guidance from the players. At a later stage she made a suggestion to encourage the group to include a less confident child.

Nursery and reception children are likely to find organised or co-operative play difficult without adult input. When providing more structured play, you are aiming to help them to learn a range of activities and games. This may require breaking down the task to enable the children to develop the necessary skills.

For example, when teaching a ball game, one LTS helped by regularly demonstrating the process in a circle. Once the children were able to catch the ball she had thrown to each one in turn, she then encouraged them to take turns to throw the ball to each other.

Often nursery and reception have separate age-appropriate playgrounds. When space is limited your school may decide to stagger the lunchtime to give the younger children time on their own.

Use of older children and buddies to support play

Children often benefit from mixing with other age-grouped pupils. Schools often recruit older buddies to interact and initiate play with the younger children. As discussed previously such schemes are likely to need careful supervision.

> **CASE STUDY 6**
>
> In one local authority, students from the local secondary schools spent time in a primary school playground at lunchtime. They taught simple games to the children and structured the play for 30 minutes, twice weekly.

Consulting children

For playgrounds to be successful, their organisation will need to be reviewed regularly and adapted. Mary Jackson (2004) says:

> Your pupils are the experts. They should be involved in playground and playtime planning from the start. But you shouldn't ask them what they *want* in the playground, or you'd get a list of things like roller coasters. You should ask the children what they would like to *do* in the playground.

> **CASE STUDY 7**
>
> In one school, the LTSs consulted the younger children about preferred activities and dressing-up clothes were requested. These were collected from a range of sources and placed in a large box in the playground. This became a great success even with some of the older classes.

Indoor play

Some children find the playground environment stressful, and schools are increasingly offering children the opportunity to attend lunchtime clubs and other indoor play provisions. Successful indoor facilities require organisation, space, staff and resources. They can offer a large range of activities including: dance, drama, chess clubs, arts and crafts, computing and languages.

A playground checklist

Does the school:	Yes	No
Review playground supervision on a regular basis?	☐	☐
Ensure all areas of the playground are supervised especially areas that are hard to see?	☐	☐
Introduce playground initiatives to create an anti-bullying ethos?	☐	☐
Provide activities to meet the needs of a range of pupils?	☐	☐
Train supervisors to initiate, teach and sustain play activities?	☐	☐
Zone the playground to decrease marginalisation or isolation of children?	☐	☐
Provide and replace a range of playground equipment?	☐	☐
Have a playground with adequate fixed equipment and markings?	☐	☐
Train supervisors to recognise and respond to bullying?	☐	☐
Have clear procedures for supervising the toilets when necessary?	☐	☐

Have enough working water fountains in the playground?	☐	☐
Have adequate shade in the playground?	☐	☐
Have reasonably clean toilets?	☐	☐
Consult children on a regular basis about the playground?	☐	☐

Every Child Matters – play at lunchtime

The table below looks at the lunchtime supervisor's role in supporting the five *ECM* outcomes when organising play at lunchtime.

ECM outcomes	The lunchtime supervisor's role in supporting the five *ECM* outcomes when organising play at lunchtime
Be healthy	Provide children with an opportunity to exercise and develop a healthy lifestyle
	Encourage children's opportunities for physical, creative, intellectual, and imaginative development through play
	Help children develop a range of social and emotional learning through structured and unstructured play
	Help children to learn to win and lose when playing competitively
Stay safe	Set clear rules for behaviour
	Plan for positive behaviour and co-operation
	Organise the playground to ensure maximum safety
	Carry out regular risk assessment in relation to activities and equipment
	Teach children to make realistic risk assessments when playing
	Display zero tolerance towards bullying and violence or antisocial behaviour
Enjoy and achieve	Provide positive and enjoyable play opportunities which offer a range of options
	Offer clear praise and rewards for positive behaviour
	Supervise activities and join in whenever appropriate
	Encourage inclusion and independence for all pupils
	Encourage pupils to have high aspirations
Make a positive contribution	Ensure pupils are consulted regularly and offer feedback on play opportunities
	Encourage children to take responsibility for their own play and behaviour
	Help children to problem solve and tackle difficulties/disagreements assertively
	Encourage pupils to include and support others
Achieve economic wellbeing	Encourage: • children to become play leaders and to contribute to lunchtimes activities • leadership, independence and teamwork • children to initiate and develop activities.

Conclusion

During lunchtime, children benefit from the opportunity to play freely and to participate in structured, organised activities. To supervise and initiate successful play at lunchtime you will need to develop a range of skills that are often not used in other aspects of your work. For some LTSs, this comes easily; others may need training and support. Find time to review your playground organisation and practice. Consider what is working well and what could be improved. A little imagination and creativity can go a long way.

Further reading and resources

For up-to-date information about play and playgrounds you can contact your local authority and ask for the PE and school sports co-ordinator.

Blatchford, Peter (1998) *Social Life in Schools: Pupils' Experience of Breaktimes and Recess from 7–16*. London: Routledge.

British Heart Foundation *Active Playgrounds: A Guide for Primary Schools* (free) (www.bhf.org.uk). Telephone 0845 0708070. In response to concerns about children's obesity levels and inactive lifestyles.

Byl, John (2003) *101 Fun Warm-up and Cool-down Games*. Human Kinetics, Europe Ltd.

Collins, Wendy (1998) *Active Playtimes* (www.southgatepublishers.co.uk).

Everyone Can Play – Inclusive play training pack.

Games Kids Play (www.gameskidsplay.net)
This is an American site that offers games from a range of countries.

Growing Schools (www.teachernet.gov.uk)
This is a major government programme to harness the full potential of the 'outdoor playground'. Pearson Publishing.

Play Work Partnership (www.playwork.co.uk)
Telephone 0870 1206466.

Golding, Rob (2000) *Playground Games. More Playground Games*. Pearson Publishing.

Healthy Lives, Brighter Futures
The strategy for children and young people's health (DCSF, February 2009).

Jackson, Mary (2004), quoted in David Bocking, 'Time for play', *TES*, 8 October 2004.

Learning through Landscapes provides a range of relevant fact sheets and information packs to members (www.ltl.org.uk). Telephone 01962 846258.

The National Play Strategy, December 2008.

Northern, Stephanie (2004) 'School grounds,' *TES*, 16 January 2004.

PE and Sports Strategy (DCSF 2008) (http://www.teachernet.gov.uk).

Bloom, Adi (2009) 'Pupils crave chance to branch out alone', *TES*, 30 January.

Play England (2008). *Play in Schools and Integrated Settings*.

Play England (www.playengland.org.uk)
A lottery funded organisation providing research, resources and training on all aspects of play (formerly the Play Council).

Playground Pals (www.pioneer.cwc.net/playgroundpals.htm)
This is a fascinating website that provides international games, case studies information about equipment and playground management.

Primary Playground Development Pack Youth Sport Trust (www.youthsporttrust.org) Telephone 01509 226600.

Thomson, Sarah (2003) 'A well equipped hamster cage: the rationalisation of primary school playtime', *Education 3–13*, June.

Thomson, Sarah (2005) 'Territorialising the primary school playground: deconstructing the geography of playtime'. *Children's Geographies*, 3(1), 63–78, April.

Titman, Wendy (1992) *Play, Playtimes and Playgrounds*. Crediton: Southgate Publishers.

Val Sabin (http://www.valsabinpublications.com/training/positive-play.php).

White, Angela and Wilkinson, Jane (2000) *Playtimes and Playgrounds*. Bristol: Lucky Duck.

Play work training

Play work training qualifications (www.Playwork.org.uk). Telephone 020 7632 2000.

The Council for Disabled Children (www.ncb.org.uk). Telephone 0207 843 6000.

Top Activity Training

An activity programme targeted at children who are reluctant to engage in sports (www.youthsporttrust.org/page/topactivity/index.html).

Training Pack. Gloucestershire: National Centre Playwork Education South West.

Youth Sport Trust (2004) *Primary Playground Development Pack*. Loughborough: Youth Sport Trust.

Equipment manufacturers

The Association of Play Industries provide a full list (www.playindustries.org) Telephone 02476 414999.

Funders

MyPlace – The Big Lottery Fund is delivering MyPlace on behalf of the Department for Children, Schools and Families (DCSF) (http://www.biglotteryfund.org.uk/prog_myplace.htm

The Lottery Fund (www.community-fund.org.uk).

Department for Culture, Media and Sport, Zoneparcs funding (www.culture.gov.uk).
The Primary Playground Programme (government funding to develop and upgrade equipment in school serving the most deprived areas).

Learning through Landscapes (www.ltl.org.uk) provides a funders list for members, *The Directory for Social Change*, see Fundraising for Schools (www.dsc.org.uk).

Managing wet play

Introduction

Lunchtime staff will know how the weather takes on a whole new meaning. On windy days, children tend to run wild. An hour and a quarter can feel like an eternity on a cold November day, worse still when there are heavy scattered showers. Do you keep the children in or let them out?

Wet play is unlikely to be an ideal situation, but can be manageable, and even enjoyable. In fact, some children welcome the option of being inside, preferring it to the rough and tumble of the playground. This chapter will explore how schools and LTSs can work together to make wet play a more positive experience. It will cover: planning, preparation, practical organisation of space and staff, and the creative use of resources and activities.

Managing wet play

Wet play is often top of LTSs' 'dislikes' list, as the challenges of managing it can be considerable. How do you cope with a hyperactive child within the confines of the classroom? How do you stay calm when trying to ensure that all children eat, are kept busy and safe, often in limited space, and possibly with an inadequate numbers of supervisors?

ACTIVITY 1

Here are some questions which will help you and your team to review the organisation of wet play. Allow yourself a few minutes on each question.

- Do you have time to plan and prepare for wet play and to review your practice?
- At what stage do you decide that it is too wet for children to be outside?
- Who decides that it is wet play and how is this communicated?
- How many classes are you required to supervise?
- During wet play, how successfully do you manage challenging behaviour?
- Where do you supervise the children?
- During wet play, what play equipment and resources do you have to keep the children occupied?

Planning and preparing for wet play

Finding time to plan wet play activities will make a real difference to the quality of the sessions. In practice, there is not a great deal of time available to plan, and some teams use INSET days for this purpose, whilst others meet briefly before or after duty. Tasks to be tackled include: reviewing existing arrangements, sorting equipment, photocopying activity sheets, or developing ideas for improvement.

Deciding it is wet play

Many schools will allow children to remain outside whilst it drizzles, although this is not always the case. Often the senior LTS or the school senior manager makes the decision to bring children inside and communicates this by using a whistle, bell, walkie-talkie or flag. Others rely on a manager or the senior LTS to tell everyone.

Supervising the dining room and the classrooms during wet play

You will need to carefully consider how many LTSs are needed to supervise the dining room, and how many this will leave to supervise the classrooms.

> **CASE STUDY 1**
>
> In one school an LTS described how, during wet play, she often had to rush between three classrooms on two different floors of the school building to supervise the children. Classes were left without adult supervision for some minutes, posing health and safety risks.

See Chapter 10 for further health and safety discussions.

> **CASE STUDY 2**
>
> In an inner-city school, relief LTSs were asked to work when it looked likely to be wet play. Although this had financial implications, the head teacher believed it to be money well spent.

ACTIVITY 2

In your school how many LTSs supervise the dining room during wet play?

Does this leave enough supervisors free to manage the rest of the school?

Can the system be improved in any way?

Discuss your ideas and concerns with your line manager.

Managing children's behaviour

Tempers are more likely to flare when children feel cooped up and frustrated. Many of the practices described in Chapters 4 and 5 are relevant in these circumstances. It will also help for the wet play rules to be clear and on display. You may need to know how to get adequate management back-up when necessary.

Where are the children supervised?

During wet play children are likely to be supervised in their own classroom. However, schools may be lucky enough to have libraries, spare classrooms or a separate dining room or hall to use. With adequate space you will have more scope to organise special activities which offer children exercise, stimulation and excitement. Without this space, you will have to work particularly hard to make the most of the existing facilities. Below are some examples of how schools have used the available space creatively.

CASE STUDY 3

Children took turns to use the hall to watch a video. Sometimes they participated in large group activities, including disco dancing, parachute games, cheerleading and team games. Those who did not wish to participate could stay in a supervised classroom.

CASE STUDY 4

Small groups of children volunteered to attend a board game club and a computer club held on rainy days in the school library and computer suite. An LTS and a learning mentor supervised the sessions.

CASE STUDY 5

Classes took turns to participate in a range of games and activities held under a weatherproof canopy in the playground, led by an LTS and a teaching assistant.

CASE STUDY 6

Volunteers from the whole of year 4 were able to attend a 30-minute craft activity held in one of their classrooms, supervised by an LTS. Those who did not wish to attend were supervised in the other classroom. On another occasion they organised a singing session in a similar way.

CASE STUDY 7

An LTS organised a game of charades for the older children in the hall. On another occasion they played 'Just a Minute' and had a balloon debate.

Clearly such activities require planning, team co-operation and careful supervision but benefits are likely to outweigh the pressures.

Keeping children occupied

With planning and imagination, there is a great deal you can do to keep children occupied. To achieve the best results you will need to:

- Build in time to plan and prepare for wet play activities
- Communicate clearly with the class teacher about the use of classroom equipment
- Create a collection of separate wet play equipment for each class
- Regularly update and swap this equipment between classes to provide novelty value
- Use your own entertainment skills
- Consider using older buddies to help with play for the younger children
- Try to ensure that the equipment and activities meet the needs of the wide range of children you supervise.

Create a wet play box

Many schools create a wet play box for each class, which is stored safely and used only on rainy days. A typical wet play box includes:

- Paper/pencils/crayons
- Word sheets/colouring sheets, dot-to-dot
- Quizzes
- Board games
- A range of books
- Comics
- Card games
- Construction toys
- Videos/DVDs.

You can make this more interesting by adding some of the following:

- Card (although this is expensive)

- Scrap boxes – collected from households and used to make models
- Plasticine and Play-Doh
- Shoe boxes filled with objects for children to write or tell stories about (see Case Study 8 below)
- Simple crossword or sudoku puzzles
- Connect Four
- Carefully selected catalogues, to be read or cut out
- Dressing-up clothes
- Miniature pool, snooker or football tables
- Sources of music
- Wool/string
- Glue/scissors, if considered to be safe
- Quizzes, and laminated sheets with water-soluble pens attached
- Traditional games, for example jacks or gobs.

Regularly update and swap the equipment between classes.

Indoor games and activities

There will be occasions when children will happily play with the equipment you provide. On other occasions you might need to initiate a specific activity or game to focus their attention or to calm them down. Some popular indoor games include:

- Simon says
- Wink murder
- Charades/acting/miming
- Noughts and crosses
- Head down thumbs up
- Hangman
- Singing games
- Memory games
- Sleeping tigers.

There are also a range of games to promote healthy eating which have been outlined in Chapter 7. Details of these and many more can be found in the play packages listed at the end of Chapter 8. More boisterous pupils will benefit from physical activities, which can be offered subject to available space. Imaginative LTSs describe a wide range of additional activities that they use during wet play to interest the children (see Case Studies 8–12):

CASE STUDY 8

An LTS put a range of unusual objects into shoeboxes; for example, a feather, a pine cone and a small mirror. Teams of children were encouraged to make up or write a story about the objects to be shared with the rest of the class. Her colleague organised a 'Show and tell' session, followed by a video for the younger children.

CASE STUDY 9

An LTS entertained children for a whole lunchtime by offering a prize for the best portrait of her. On other occasions she organised competitions, including timed puzzles using a stop watch, a talent competition, 'draw the best cartoon character' and 'design a poster to promote healthy eating'. The children helped her to judge the best efforts and winners were awarded a small prize by the class teacher.

CASE STUDY 10

A group of year 6 children were allowed to dance to their own music in the classroom, provided the noise level remained reasonable. When things became rowdy, a game of wink murder was initiated.

CASE STUDY 11

Children were encouraged to make Winter Festival cards using card, glue sticks and magazine cuttings. Others were taught to fold paper to make simple animals and boats.

CASE STUDY 12

A group of reception children played a range of games such as 'oranges and lemons' and 'the farmer's in the den' in one half of the classroom. Later, they sang along with a nursery rhyme tape and played memory games.

Use your own entertainment skills

You are the most important resource available to the children. Think carefully about the particular skills you may have. Can you play chess or a musical instrument? Can you sing or make paper models? You do not need to be an expert to have a go; children are likely to respond to your ideas and enthusiasm.

Use the older buddies to help with play for the younger children

A number of schools use their buddies to assist during wet play. You will need to oversee their involvement and provide clear tasks. Never leave older buddies alone in a classroom to supervise younger pupils though.

Ensure that the equipment and activities meet the needs of the wide range of children you supervise

This is never easy, as the majority of children usually would prefer to be playing outside. Ask them how they experience wet play and what could improve things. When choosing equipment and activities, as always you will need to consider the age of the children, the needs of the boys and the girls, as well as children with special needs. It is also advisable to select books, comics, dressing-up clothes and music that reflect a range of cultures.

ACTIVITY 3

Think of the children you find particularly difficult to keep occupied during wet play. Do they fit into a particular group? (For example, are they: boys, girls, children of a particular age group, or children with special needs?)

Is there someone at school who could offer advice about these difficulties?

Every Child Matters during wet play

Many of the points listed in the *ECM* table at the end of Chapter 8 are also applicable to wet play.

Conclusion

Wet play need not dampen your spirits. There is a lot you can do to make it a more positive experience for all involved. Hopefully, some of the ideas outlined in this chapter will help you to become more confident and adventurous in your wet play activities.

Keeping children safe and healthy at lunchtime

Introduction

> There is no such thing as a completely safe play environment because there is no such thing as a safe child! Children will have accidents wherever they are. They will fall over each other, their feet and even over nothing at all.

(Titman 1992)

During lunchtime, you are often dealing with large numbers of children who have been inside for several hours and have lots of energy. The concept of danger seems alien to many, and you are required to stop them doing things they desperately want to do. It is not surprising that, when attempting to keep children physically safe, you can sometimes feel like a 'moaning Minnie'.

This chapter will explore measures you and your school can take to keep children safe at lunchtime in the playground and inside the school building. Your legal responsibilities will be outlined, as well as your role when assessing and managing risk, coping with accidents, administering first aid, recording incidents and dealing with pupils' special needs.

Legal responsibilities

All school staff have a legal responsibility to keep themselves and others safe. The Health and Safety at Work Act 1974 places overall responsibility for health and safety on the

employers. In schools, this is shared by the local authority, the governors and the head teacher. If you wish to find out more, see Notes for managers, page 143.

As employees, LTSs have a responsibility to:

- Take reasonable care of their own health and safety whilst at work, and the health and safety of others who may be affected by their acts (including the children)
- Co-operate with their employers in health and safety matters
- Carry out activities in accordance with training and instruction
- Inform their employer of any serious risk.

Understanding your health and safety policy

By law, employers must have a health and safety policy that outlines measures to be taken to assess and manage risk. Schools are expected to make employees aware of their roles and responsibilities. If you have not already got a copy, request summaries and guidelines relevant to keeping children safe at lunchtime.

Risk assessment

What is risk assessment?

As part of your job you will be required to assess risks and take measures to reduce them. Whenever there are groups of people there will be an element of risk, as accidents can happen in almost any situation. Assessing risk involves deciding on the *likelihood* of an accident occurring within a particular set of circumstances. For example; you are likely to decide that letting children run in the playground is a low risk activity, whilst letting children run in the dining room is high risk. Consequently, you would expect to prevent children running in the dining room, but not in the playground.

To make good assessments about levels of risk, you will need to use common sense and life experience as well as some specialist knowledge, as demonstrated by the following example:

CASE STUDY 1

During wet play, an LTS removed a jar of buttons from the reach of the nursery children as she decided there was a high risk that they would put the objects in their mouths and possibly choke. With the junior school classes, she did not assess this as a high risk, so did not remove the jar, unless she was supervising a class that included children with special needs.

In this example, the LTS used her knowledge of child development, special educational needs and first aid to assess risk. In practice, you are making these assessments every day.

Keeping children safe in the playground and the school building

The playground

In the playground large numbers of children move around relatively freely, and so accidents *do* happen. It is not surprising that LTSs may find that keeping children safe is stressful. One LTS described the pressure: 'I hate moaning and spoiling their fun, but looking after other people's children is such a serious responsibility. I feel sick at the thought of a child being seriously injured.'

There is a fine line between ensuring safety in the playground and allowing children to play freely. As described in Chapter 8, it is normal for children to experiment and to stretch their own physical limits. Children vary in their understanding of danger and in their level of physical ability. When supervising them, it is tempting to err on the side of caution. This, too, can create problems.

In a survey of 90,000 pupils conducted by Play England, more than than three quarters of the participants said they would like more opportunities to take risks while playing. The survey reveals that pupils are more than 100 times less likely to injure themselves in the playground than by playing organised sport, such as rugby. Tim Gill, of Play England, said: 'We don't live in a risk-free world. One of the things that helps children discover the consequences of their actions is when things go wrong, or when they see other children have accidents' (Adi Bloom, *TES*, 30 January 2009).

> Play provision that is stimulating, challenging and exciting allows children to take risks, which helps them to build confidence, learn skills and develop resilience at their own pace...It also helps them to manage risk safely in their lives.
>
> (Play England 2008)

Thomson (2003) warns against a worrying trend in primary school playgrounds, mainly in response to health and safety concerns and fear of prosecution. She believes that staff are becoming over-protective and controlling, and that schools often have the philosophy, 'when in doubt ban it'. This has sometimes resulted in the banning of activities like football, skipping, rounders, yo-yos, playing with conkers and wearing certain types of shoes. She fears that playgrounds are becoming 'barren, sterile and unimaginative places' and that spontaneous play, choice, creativity and fun are being unnecessarily stifled.

Find a balance between keeping children safe in the playground, whilst allowing them to play in an exciting and challenging way.

advice

Other environmental factors that affect children's health and safety at lunchtime

Children require sufficient shade and drinking water to avoid the risk of sunburn or dehydration. The design and size of your playground may create potential dangers, especially if there are hidden corners, or dangerous structures such as spiked fences and sheds with flat roofs to climb on. Accidents can be caused by broken play equipment, which will require regular inspection. Insecure playground boundaries and playgrounds with public access can also add to difficulties, especially if gates are left open and uninvited visitors enter the playground. For further discussion about playground security see Notes for managers, page 144.

ACTIVITY 1

Think about the playground you supervise. In the first column list examples of possible risks to children's safety in the playground at lunchtime. In the second column identify action that you or others take to reduce the risks.

Discuss your answers with your colleagues and line manager.

Risks to the children's safety in the playground	Action taken to reduce risk
Example:	
Faulty equipment, for example a splintered wooden bat or a broken climbing frame	I regularly check equipment and remove faulty goods. In the case of broken equipment, I stop children using it and report this to the caretaker immediately to be fenced off and repaired.
	Continue until you have eight examples.

Your answers might include:

- Under-supervised areas of the playground – for example, a hidden corner which can be overlooked

  Action: Be vigilant and agree as a team how best to manage the problem. If difficulties remain, discuss these with your line manager.

- Children playing in a rough way

  Action: Learn to identify safe and unsafe play – see Chapters 6 and 8, pages 61 and 84. Intervene when necessary. Remind children about the school rules about play.

- Unsuitable equipment

  Action: To avoid injury, children should be using soft balls instead of leather balls. This needs to be monitored and children need reminders in assembly.

- Unclear playground rules – for example, children are not consistently challenged when they climb on fences, buildings and other 'forbidden' structures

  Action: Act consistently and remind children of playground rules. Expectations may need to be reinforced by senior managers.

- Poor security, including: a public right of way through your playground, gates that are left open, or gaps in the fence where objects can be passed to the children.

  Action: With the help of senior managers, reinforce the importance of playground safety to parents/carers. Politely challenge uninvited visitors in the playground, and direct them to the school office. Call for assistance if necessary.

- Unsafe car parking facilities; children and vehicles sometimes share the same playground

  Action: Monitor carefully and feed back concerns to senior managers regularly.

 If you are worried that issues are not being acted upon, keep on voicing your concerns until you are satisfied with the outcome.

Keeping children safe in the school building

LTSs supervise children in the dining room and in their classrooms during wet play. You may also supervise them in the medical room or during lunchtime clubs and detentions.

In the dining room

To enhance safety, schools can provide clear rules and routines for queuing, eating and the disposal of left-over food. Everyone must know who is responsible for sweeping food from the floor and mopping up spilt drinks. There will need to be clear expectations about how children enter the dining room and where they sit. Children care as much about sitting with their friends as they do about what they eat, and you will need to strike a balance between keeping them safe whilst allowing them to socialise and eat together in a relaxed atmosphere.

During wet play

During wet play, you may have to leave children unsupervised in the classroom for short periods whilst attending to other classes. This is a cause for concern to be discussed with your line manager. Wet play equipment requires regular inspection and activities will need to be planned and monitored carefully. Try to consider the possible risks in advance and think of ways to reduce them. Activities may need to be stopped, amended or cancelled if they appear to be too dangerous or you have an insufficient number of adults to supervise them.

ACTIVITY 2

Think about the times you supervise children inside the school building at lunchtime.

In the first column list several examples of possible risks to the children's safety during lunchtime? In the second column identify action that you or others can take to reduce risk.

Discuss your answer with colleagues/line manager.

Risks to the children's safety inside the school at lunchtime	Action to be taken to reduce risk
Example:	
Children running into the dining room	I challenge them and remind them clearly of the school rule about running. Teaching staff also reinforce this in assembly and in the classroom.
	Continue until you have eight examples.

Listed risks and actions may include:

- Unacceptable behaviour in the dining room including running, shouting, pushing or poor table manners

  Action: Challenge assertively and refer children to the dining room rules.

- Hazards due to food and drink on the dining room floor

  Action: Agree on clear procedures about sweeping and mopping the floor.

- Unclear rules and routine for moving around the school building. For example, children run up and down stairs when coming inside from the playground

  Action: Challenge this and clarify your expectations. Request that expectations are reinforced by senior managers and teaching staff.

- Children entering the building having been given permission by teaching staff without your knowledge. This is obviously dangerous as they may be unsupervised, or unaccounted for in the case of an emergency.

  Action: Discuss with your line manager to ensure that systems are in place to stop this happening.

- Faulty equipment or dangerous activities during wet play

  Action: Check equipment regularly and monitor the safety of activities.

● Insufficient numbers of LTSs to supervise classrooms during wet play

   Action: Discuss your concerns with your line manager and review wet play arrangements regularly.

Training in health and safety matters

Your employer is required under health and safety law to provide training to ensure that you are competent to carry out your responsibilities. This may involve attending external courses or receiving school-based instruction. *Guidance for Safer Working Practice for Adults who Work with Children and Young People* (HSE 2007) states:

> It is expected that adults working with children and young people should be aware of basic first aid techniques. It is not, however, a contractual requirement and whilst adults may volunteer to undertake such tasks, they should be suitably trained and qualified before administering first aid and/or any agreed medication.

Children can also benefit from training in how to avoid accidents, in first aid and in resuscitation skills. The government intends to set up a Child Safety Education Coalition to focus on practical safety education for children in England.

Coping with accidents and emergencies

Even in well managed, safety-conscious schools, accidents will happen. Having clear roles, procedures and well prepared competent staff can reduce the risk of harm being caused. To avoid panic and confusion, anticipate and discuss in advance how best to respond to various types of accidents and emergencies.

As illustrated by the following true incidents, school playgrounds are unpredictable places where exciting and amusing, as well as tragic, incidents take place.

● Much to the excitement of the children and staff, an emergency helicopter was forced to land in the junior school playground at home time, following a serious road accident nearby.

● A completely naked, mentally unwell man ran through a primary school playground, being hotly pursued by two uniformed police officers.

● A wild and dangerous-looking dog managed to gain access to the playground at lunchtime, terrifying the children.

● A child became physically stuck in the playground climbing frame and had to be rescued by the fire brigade.

ACTIVITY 3

List several types of emergencies that you may be required to deal with.

1

2

3

4

5

6

Discuss with colleagues how you would respond to each of these situations.

When considering appropriate action, do you know:

How to raise the fire alarm?

Where the school fire exits are situated?

Set procedures for evacuating the school building?

How to access children's medical records when necessary?

How to administer basic first aid?

How to call for assistance when necessary?

Whose responsibility it is to call the ambulance?

How to challenge 'difficult' visitors to the playground

How to record accidents and illnesses.

 If you are unclear about any of these points, seek clarification.

Fire procedures

All LTSs will need to be clear about the schools fire procedures. Fire evacuation during wet play would be particularly problematic to manage as all the children would be inside the building. If your school does not practise their fire drill during lunchtime because of the disruption it causes, you can suggest creating a mock scenario to practise these procedures (see Notes for managers, page 145).

Offering children reassurance

During and after emergencies, children who have been directly involved or who have witnessed distressing incidents are likely to need considerable comfort and reassurance. Some relevant skills have been outlined in Chapter 3. Children will differ greatly in the way they deal with their feelings and if you are unsure how best to respond, seek advice or refer the child on to someone appropriate.

Fist aid training

Your school is required to provide adequate and appropriate equipment, facilities and qualified first aid personnel for providing first aid in the school. They must also inform all staff of the first aid arrangements.

LTSs are often offered basic first aid training to enable them to respond confidently to common illness and routine incidents. You may also receive instruction about how best to lift heavy equipment, and to deal with infection and children's bodily functions. LTSs need to know who the appointed first aiders are, and when to pass on more serious matters to be dealt with. You will also require clear guidelines about dealing with children with special medical needs and disabilities, as well as issues relating to infection control and the use of medication, including creams and plasters. You may be invited by the school to train to become a qualified first aider. This entails completing and updating in-depth, approved first aid training. Duties include:

● Giving immediate help to casualties with common injuries or illnesses and those arising from hazards at school

● When necessary, ensuring that an ambulance or other professional medical help is summoned.

A government good practice guide entitled *Guidance on First Aid for Schools 1998* (DfES 1998b) outlines roles and responsibilities in considerable detail.

ACTIVITY 4

Part A

Can you identify the qualified first aiders in your school?

Do you feel you have you been offered adequate first aid training?

Do you have discussions about how to respond to children's minor or major accidents?

Part B

Discuss the following true case study. With hindsight, how should this accident have been dealt with?

CASE STUDY 2

A child collided with another in the playground at lunchtime, hitting her head and losing consciousness briefly. She then came round, sat up, lost consciousness again for a few seconds, came round again and stood up. The LTSs on duty made the decision to escort her to the welfare room. The welfare officer was new to the school and had very little first aid training. She was not informed at this stage that the child had lost consciousness twice in the playground. She phoned the child's mother and explained that her daughter had had an accident and needed to be collected. The mother arrived promptly, and although her daughter was able to walk to the car, she lost consciousness some minutes later. The mother later prosecuted the LEA for negligence.

Learning points from this incident:

● The child should not have been moved from the playground as she had suffered a potentially serious injury

● An ambulance should have been called immediately, either by an LTS or the welfare officer. It could have been cancelled later, if no longer needed

● The LTSs and the welfare officer should have had adequate first aid training

● The welfare officer should have been called to the playground and given full details of what had happened

● The mother should have been given full details about what had happened.

Recording and reporting accidents

By law, schools are required to record accidents in writing, usually in an accident book, although in more serious cases a local authority or government accident form may also need to be completed. Following accidents, you will also be required to inform other relevant members of staff as soon as possible, so that they can decide if there is further action to be taken. You can do this by word of mouth and by filling in an accident form. The information is often confidential and should only be discussed with the relevant people. If parents or carers approach you, unless you have been advised otherwise, refer them to the class teacher or senior manager.

Schools, by law, are required to report all serious injuries and some diseases to the Health and Safety Executive (HSE). The HSE enforces health and safety law relating to the activities of local authorities and schools. For more information visit http://www.hse.gov.uk/

Supporting pupils with specific medical needs

Schools have a responsibility under the Disability Discrimination Act 1995 to ensure pupils with medical needs have access to all aspects of school life. Some pupils will have medical conditions that require support so that they can attend school regularly. Your school is likely to have a policy on managing pupils' medicine and on supporting their medical needs. Generally, schools do not administer medication, although exceptions may be made in special cases. You will need to obtain sufficient medical information about the pupils in your care, and children with long-term or significant medical conditions should have a medical needs healthcare plan which outlines what they need to keep them safe and well. You may also require specialist training in a range of areas including: responding to fits, using asthma pumps and epipens (necessary in some cases of severe allergic reactions). For more detailed information seek guidance from specialist staff. You can also read *Managing Medicine in Schools and Early Years Settings* (DfES 2005b).

When things go wrong

Sadly, things do occasionally go wrong and, in extreme cases, legal action may be taken against an LEA or school. Between 2007 and 2008 almost two million pounds were paid in compensation to parents, following, mainly, playground accidents. The majority of these were caused by falls or collisions (*The Telegraph* on line, July 2008). Although it is rare, in theory, action can be taken against individuals too. It is therefore crucial that you co-operate with your employers in health and safety matters and carry out activities in accordance with training and instruction. If legal problems arise for employees, unions are an important source of advice.

Keeping yourself safe and healthy

Responsibility for looking after children and keeping them safe can be stressful. It is crucial that you also look after yourself at work and receive the necessary support and training to help you cope. This has been discussed in previous chapters and will be revisited in Chapter 11.

Every Child Matters – keeping children safe

The table below looks at the lunchtime supervisor's role in supporting the five *ECM* outcomes when keeping children safe at lunchtime.

ECM outcomes	The lunchtime supervisor's role in supporting the five *ECM* outcomes when keeping children safe at lunchtime
Be healthy	Follow health and safety policy and procedure
	Undertake all relevant first aid and health and other safety training
	Be aware of signs and symptoms of ill health or injury
	Obtain up-to-date information about children's medical issues, dietary needs, allergies, eating issues and special educational needs
	Encourage children to make healthy lifestyle choices
	Communicate with others on a need to know basis

Stay safe	Set clear and safe rules in relation to behaviour
	Respond to accidents, emergencies and ill health in line with school policy and procedures
	Practise procedures for evacuating the school building and the fire drill procedures at lunchtime
	Inspect all equipment regularly
	Be proactive – anticipate risk and respond appropriately
	Organise the playground dining room and classrooms to ensure maximum safety
	Follow school procedures in relation to appropriate physical contact with pupils
	Record all incidents in line with school policy
	Consider how to challenge unauthorised playground visitors
	Be clear how to call for emergency assistance when necessary
	Display zero tolerance towards bullying and violence or antisocial behaviour
Enjoy and achieve	Create a positive lunchtime ethos
	Provide enjoyable play opportunities that offer a range of options
	Encourage inclusion and independence for all pupils
	Encourage pupils to embrace new experiences
Make a positive contribution	Ensure pupils are consulted regularly and offer feedback on lunchtime issues
	Encourage children to take responsibility for their own play and behaviour
	Help children to problem solve and tackle difficulties/disagreements
	Teach children to make realistic risk assessments when undertaking activities
	Encourage children to reflect on and take responsibility for their actions
Achieve economic wellbeing	Encourage children to initiate and contribute to lunchtimes activities
	Encourage leadership, independence and teamwork
	Help pupils to develop risk assessment skills.

Conclusion

This chapter clarifies your role and responsibilities when keeping children safe at lunchtime. Although thinking about accidents and emergencies can make people feel anxious, it helps to remember that serious accidents and emergencies in schools are rare, and that LTSs usually do an excellent job when it comes to caring for and protecting children.

Further information and reading

Bloom, Adi (2009) 'Pupils crave chance to branch out alone', *TES*, 30 January.

Child Safety Education Coalition (http://www.csec.org.uk/).

DCSF (2007) *Guidance for Safer Working Practice for Adults Who Work with Children and Young People.*

DCSF (2008) *Staying Safe: Action Plan.*

DCSF school security website – www.dcsf.gov.uk/schoolsecurity

DfES (1998b) *Guidance on First Aid for School: A Good Practice Guide.* Teachernet website.

DfES (2001) *Health and Safety Responsibilities and Powers.* London: DfES.

DfES (2005a) *Playtimes and Lunchtimes: Primary National Strategy Professional Development Pack.* London: DfES.

DfES (2005b) *Managing Medicine in Schools and Early Years Settings.* Teachernet website.

The Health and Safety Executive (HSE) (http://www.hse.gov.uk/)
Enforces health and safety law relating to the activities of local authorities and schools.

Lloyd, Richard and Ching, Charlene (2003) *School Security Concerns.* Teachernet website.

Play England (2008) *Play in Schools and Integrated Settings.*

Teachernet website (www.teachernet.gove.uk) – provides a comprehensive list of up to date and relevant health and safety guidelines and information.

Thomson, Sarah (2003) 'A well equipped hamster cage: the rationalisation of primary school playtime', *Education 3–13*, June.

The Telegraph on line (telegraph.co.uk) (2008) 'Almost 2 million paid in playground accident claim', July.

Titman, Wendy (1992) *Play, Playtimes and Playgrounds.* Crediton: Southgate Publishers.

Safeguarding children

Introduction

Sadly, there are likely to be children in your school who are being abused. They may choose to tell you, as a trusted person, about their unhappiness and mistreatment, or they may not. Support staff are often working closely with children, sometimes in intimate situations, and so may be in the 'front line' in detecting abuse. This chapter will explore how to recognise the signs and how best to respond to protect children. It will examine your role and responsibilities, and explain how to protect yourself from false accusations of abuse at work.

Information about child abuse

What is child abuse?

Abuse is when a child or young person under the age of 18 is hurt or harmed by another person in a way that causes, or is likely to cause, significant harm and which may well have an effect on their development or wellbeing.

When learning about or dealing with child abuse, people often experience a range of powerful emotions including anger, disgust, sadness, depression and powerlessness. The idea and the reality of child abuse is often so dreadful that it is little wonder that school staff become emotionally involved, and sometimes deny that it is actually happening. You may find this subject distressing, particularly if you have experienced abuse personally. If so, it is advisable to seek support from someone you trust.

Who abuses children?

Child abuse takes place in every social class, race and religion. Statistics suggest approximately 90 per cent of all incidents are committed by someone the child knows, often within the family. Strangers do abuse children, but far less than is usually thought to be the case.

Sexual abuse is usually carried out by men, although women and teenagers also abuse children, usually within the home. Statistics suggest there is a greater risk of child abuse in families where parents or carers have a drug or alcohol problem or where there is domestic violence. (London Child Protection Procedure 2007.)

Cultural difference

The way we raise and discipline our children will vary depending on our family and cultural rules. When working in a multicultural school, you may notice such differences. For example, in certain societies it is normal to beat children as a form of discipline, whereas in England and Wales it is unlawful to hit children in a way that reddens their skin. People will need to understand and abide by the child protection laws of their country of residence.

Safeguarding children and the law

> Children have a fundamental right to be protected from harm and abuse. All school staff have a duty of care and an important part to play in helping to protect children.
>
> (DfES 2003)

The Children Act (1989) states that the welfare of the child is paramount, and outlines the responsibilities of the local authority, schools and other organisations to ensure that children are protected from abuse. The Education Act 2002 and the Children Act 2004 outline the duty on local authorities to improve the wellbeing and to safeguard and promote the welfare of children. The DCSF document *Safeguarding Children and Safer Recruitment in Education* (2006) replaces the DfES document *Safeguarding Children in Education* (September 2004), and provides current information and guidance for schools in England.

Following the tragedy of the death of Baby P in Haringey, Lord Laming has made 58 recommendations, some of which are likely to affect school practice. *The Protection of Children in England: A Progress Report* (Laming 2009).

Procedures in school

Safer staff recruitment

All staff working with children are required to have a Criminal Records Bureau (CRB) check. In response to the Soham murders, the government has introduced the Vetting and Barring Scheme (VBS) to ensure that all staff working with children are checked and shown to be suitable. This will go fully live in 2010 and specific guidance and training material will be published in June 2009. For more information visit www.everychildmatters.gov.uk

Your school's child protection policy

Schools are required to produce a child protection policy which outlines responsibilities and procedures for protecting children. This should include how to identify, respond to, report and record concerns. All staff should be given a written statement about the school's policies and procedures, and the name of the person to whom concerns should be reported (see below).

The designated senior person for child protection

Schools are required to appoint one or more 'designated persons' from the senior management team (often, but not always, the head teacher) who have special responsibilities for dealing with child protection within the school. They are also responsible for advising staff and liaising with outside agencies.

Duty to refer

All school staff have a duty to report suspected abuse. You are *not* required to decide if the child is telling the truth, nor to investigate what has happened. Even if you feel uncertain or confused about a situation you are required to discuss your concerns or suspicions immediately. In some schools, LTSs are expected to refer concerns to the senior LTS, where as in others, it may be the class teacher or senior designated person.

The fact that you have reported your concerns will be kept confidential, and schools often introduce procedures to ensure that you remain anonymous

If you are worried that appropriate action is not being taken, request feedback and state your concerns again. Your school has a responsibility to listen to you and to take your communication seriously.

What is likely to happen if a child is referred to social services?

If serious suspicions of abuse come to light, this will be reported to the social service department by the appropriate person. Social workers are trained to interview children in specialised ways. If, following investigation, serious concerns remain, there are a number of options that can be taken. For further information you can obtain a free copy of *What to Do if You are Worried that a Child Is Being Abused* (www.everychildmatters.gov.uk and www.teachernet.gov.uk/publications or DCSF Publications, Tel: 0845 60 222 60).

Sharing information about children who have been abused

Unless you are directly involved, you are unlikely to know which children are being investigated by the social services or monitored by the school. This confidential information will only be shared with a small number of staff on a needs to know basis.

LTSs often complain that they are kept in the dark and that they would benefit from more information. One LTS spoke on behalf of her colleagues by saying: 'We don't need all the details, as we realise they are private. It would help to know which children are having serious problems. Then we could understand their behaviour better and make allowances.'

 If you are given insufficient information about the children you work with, talk to your line manager.

Safeguarding children training

All staff working in schools should be provided with training in safeguarding children relevant to their role. For LTSs, this could include guidance on how to:

- Recognise the signs of child abuse
- Listen to children
- Respond to concerns about a child's wellbeing as outlined by the school child protection policy
- Behave professionally at work to protect yourself from accusations of abuse.

Recognising the signs of abuse

When working with children, you will need to know what signs and symptoms are indicators of abuse.

ACTIVITY 1

Can you name the four categories of child abuse?

They are: physical abuse, sexual abuse, neglect and emotional abuse.

Physical abuse

Definition

> Physical abuse may involve hitting, shaking, kicking, punching, scalding, suffocating and otherwise causing physical harm to a child.
>
> Physical harm may also be caused when a parent fabricates the symptoms of, or deliberately induces, illness in a child. This is known as fabricated or induced illness. It also includes female genital mutilation (female circumcision).
>
> (London Child Protection Procedures (2007)

Physical abuse is sometimes known as 'non-accidental injury'.

Signs and symptoms

You may see marks on a child's body which are in unusual places and so are less likely to have been caused by an accident. For example, marks inside the child's thighs, behind the ears or around the groin. The shape of the marks can also give you clues. For example, they may resemble finger marks, burns, bites or those caused by straps or other objects. When you are tending to a child, they may appear to be scared, as if waiting for the next attack, or have a tendency to unexpectedly flinch away from you for no obvious reason.

Children may directly tell you that they have been abused. This is known as a 'disclosure'.

CASE STUDY 1

An LTS saw a large bruise on a child's neck, partially concealed by his shirt. When she asked how it occurred, the child said, 'My uncle punched me'. The LTS listened carefully to the child's explanation and then immediately informed her line manager.

Sexual abuse

Definition

Sexual abuse involves forcing or enticing a child or young person to take part in sexual activities, including prostitution, whether or not the child is aware of what is happening. The activities may involve physical contact, including penetrative (e.g. rape, buggery or oral sex) or non-penetrative acts. Sexual abuse includes abuse of children through sexual exploitation. Sexual abuse includes non-contact activities, such as involving children in looking at, or in the production of pornographic materials, watching sexual activities or encouraging children to behave in sexually inappropriate ways.

(London Child Protection procedures (2007)

Signs and symptoms

You may become concerned that a child's behaviour has become sexual in nature. They may touch you or other children inappropriately, act out adult sexual behaviour, draw inappropriate pictures or say inappropriate things. You may get the feeling that 'something isn't quite right' and start to feel uncomfortable. Trust these feelings and report your concerns to the appropriate person without delay. Other signs to monitor are unexpected changes in a child's behaviour including them becoming withdrawn, aggressive, anxious or tearful. Sexually abused children may also develop a range of physical symptoms including urinary tract infections, frequent headaches, stomach pains and bedwetting. They may self-harm, misuse substances such as glue or other solvents, or develop eating disorders.

Neglect

Definition

Neglect is the persistent failure to meet a child's basic physical and/or psychological needs, likely to result in the serious impairment of the child's health or development. Neglect may occur during pregnancy as a result of maternal substance abuse. It may involve a parent failing to: provide adequate food, clothing or shelter, protect a child from physical and emotional harm or danger, ensure adequate supervision, and ensure access to appropriate medical care.

(London Child Protection procedures (2007)

Signs and symptoms

Children have the right to be fed, kept warm and cared for so that they can grow into healthy adolescents and adults. Neglect is the denial of these needs. Indicators can include: children who are hungry, smelly, unkempt, dirty, constantly tired, inappropriately dressed, poor school attenders or who have untreated medical problems.

When working with children at school, we may have differing standards in relation to hygiene, appropriate clothing, healthy food and cleanliness. For example, you may be concerned that a child is wearing the same t-shirt for several days, or that his lunch box contains 'unhealthy' food. Although these concerns should be passed on, it does not necessarily mean a child is being neglected.

Here is one lunchtime supervisor's account of a child who *was* being neglected:

A year 2 child came to school regularly with a filthy lunchbox containing a few slices of mouldy bread. The child was clearly hungry and I reported this to the head teacher immediately. I was told that the social services are involved with the family and I was asked to keep a written record of the content of the child's lunch on a daily basis.

Emotional abuse

Definition

Emotional abuse is the persistent emotional maltreatment of a child such as to cause severe and persistent effects on the child's emotional development, and may involve:

> Conveying to children that they are worthless or unloved, inadequate, or valued only insofar as they meet the needs of another person; It may also involve: imposing age or developmentally inappropriate expectations on children; seeing or hearing the ill-treatment of another; serious bullying, causing children frequently to feel frightened or in danger, or the exploiting and corrupting of children.
>
> Some level of emotional abuse is involved in all types of maltreatment of a child, though it may occur alone.

> (London Child Protection procedures (2007)

Signs and symptoms

Often children who have been emotionally abused will display severe behavioural difficulties. They are likely to have very low self-esteem and to be unable to form relationships with others. These children may bully, be socially isolated or display extreme attention-seeking behaviour. They are also likely to develop physical problems similar to those described in relation to sexually abused children.

One LTS described a reception child who fitted this category:

> I am often completely at loss about what to do to help her. She is rude, violent towards others, and all over the place. Although her behaviour often makes me feel very cross, I look at this tiny little person and it also makes me really sad – I can't imagine what she's been through.

Domestic abuse/violence

Children who witness domestic abuse within the home are considered to be experiencing emotionally abuse. There is a strong likelihood that men who are violent to women are also likely to be violent towards children. If a child talks about domestic abuse within the family, report it without delay.

Listening to children

As outlined in Chapter 3, LTSs will be required to listen to children in an open, non-judgemental and enabling way. You will also need to know how to respond sensitively to a child's concerns, whom to approach for advice and that you cannot guarantee complete confidentiality.

How children may tell you about abuse

Children might inform you about the abuse they are suffering in a number of ways. They might make a straightforward statement and describe what is happening, make comments or ask you questions. They may hint that something is wrong, talk about something bad happening to a friend or communicate this to you in a non-verbal way through their play or actions. Try to be sensitive to these communications and seek advice if you are unsure.

When a child tells you about abuse, you should:

- Listen carefully without asking leading questions, giving your opinion, or putting words into the child's mouth
- Accept what the child is telling you. You do not have to decide if it is true or not
- Respond as calmly as possible
- Support and reassure the child, e.g. 'You have been brave to tell me. It's not your fault'
- Assume they may have been threatened

- Inform the child of what you will do and who you will need to tell
- Inform the appropriate person and follow school procedures

You should not:

- Make promises that you cannot keep; for example: 'Everything will be OK'
- Quiz the child about what happened; it is not your job to investigate
- Promise that you will keep what you have been told secret (see below)
- Tell the child you do not believe them
- Make any contact with the parent or carer – this is usually social services' responsibility
- Discuss the case with unauthorised people. If parents ask for confidential information, refer them to an appropriate member of staff.

Never keep secrets

ACTIVITY 2

How would you deal with the following situation?

> **CASE STUDY 2**
>
> A year 6 girl says that she would like to tell you about something 'bad happening to her' but will only do so if you promise not to tell anyone else. You explain why you can not make this promise and encourage the child to tell you anyway. The child refuses to say any more.

Children may ask you to keep secrets. They may have been threatened by their abuser or told that what is happening must not be talked about. You will need to explain that if they are being harmed, you must pass it on, so that they can be helped. Children usually accept this. In the above case study, you will need to encourage the child to talk by trying a range of strategies. You could explain that you are unable to help if you don't know what is happening, and could praise the child's bravery for talking to you in the first place. You could reassure her that what she says will not be the source of gossip. You could ask the child if there was anyone else she would be able to talk to, and show her that you understand how hard it can be to trust others.

You must report such discussions to an appropriate person even if you are not given any more information (see 'Duty to refer' on page 147).

Recording incidents of abuse

Your school will have clear procedures for recording incidents of abuse and storing sensitive written information. You will be required to write down the facts of what you saw or were told as soon as possible, using the child's own words when appropriate. If you find writing difficult, you can request assistance. The record should be signed, dated and kept in a confidential place.

Helping children to become aware of their personal safety

There is a great deal you and your school can do to help children to become more assertive, and to resist unhelpful pressures. Ideas have already been discussed in previous chapters. If you wish to learn more, talk to your line manager or SENCO.

Professional conduct and appropriate physical contact

To ensure high professional standards, and to avoid being subject of unfounded accusations, you will need to think carefully about how you conduct yourself at work.

ACTIVITY 3

Identify situations at work when you may be particularly vulnerable to being falsely accused of abuse. What precautions do you take to minimise the risk?

LTSs need to take particular care to follow relevant school policies and guidelines in relation to:

● Offering children intimate care
● Appropriate physical contact with pupils.

Offering children intimate care

You may be required to care for pupils intimately including those who have had toileting accidents or have been physically injured. If you work in special schools you may also be required to care intimately for pupils with disabilities. To avoid leaving yourself vulnerable, you will need to know and to follow relevant school policies, codes of conduct and guidelines, make sure other staff are aware of the task being undertaken and explain to the child what is happening. *Guidance for Safer Working Practice for Adults who Work with Children and Young People* (DCSF 2007).

Appropriate physical contact

Lunchtime staff often express uncertainty about what is expected of them in this area. On occasions they feel advice given by their line manager conflicts with their ability to do their job. A clear school policy offering guidance about appropriate physical contact is recommended, and ultimately you must be guided by your head teacher.

Government guidelines accept that school staff may choose to touch children if they are in distress and need physical comforting. Staff should be aware that some children may be particularly sensitive to physical contact as a result of their cultural background or personal experiences.

The government states that:

> There may be occasions where a distressed pupil needs comfort and reassurance which may include physical comforting such as a caring parent would give. Staff should use their discretion in such cases to ensure that what is normal and natural does not become unnecessary and unjustified contact, particularly with the same pupil over a period of time. Where a member of staff has particular concern about the need to provide this type of care and reassurance they should seek the advice of the head teacher... Adults should use their professional judgement to comfort or reassure a child in an age-appropriate way while maintaining clear professional boundaries.

(As outlined on the Teachernet website (www.teachernet.co.uk – physical contact)

The DCSF states that:

- Be circumspect in offering reassurance in one to one situations, but always record such actions in these circumstances
- Follow professional guidance or code of practice where available
- Never touch a child in a way which may be considered indecent
- Record and report situations which may give rise to concern from either party
- Not assume that all children seek physical comfort if they are distressed
- Avoid meetings with a child or young person in remote, secluded areas
- Always inform other colleagues and/or parents/carers about the contact(s) beforehand, assessing the need to have them present or close by.

(DCSF 2007)

Although some schools strongly discourage physical contact between LTSs and the children, many head teachers and LEAs recommend that physical contact should be initiated by the child and that you should never kiss or cuddle children, nor allow them to sit on your lap. You should also encourage children to dress and undress themselves, keeping the door open, and having two members of staff present when you examine or care intimately for children.

Restraint

During lunchtime you have a responsibility to keep children safe. However, it is crucial that you do not hurt a child in your attempt to protect others, or when you have lost your temper. As discussed in Chapter 6, the Education and Inspections Act 2006 enables school staff to use such force as is reasonable in the circumstances in a range of situations. The head teacher has the right to limit the power to apply particular sanctions to certain staff and schools are advised to create their own policy on the use of reasonable force to control or restrain pupils, including how to break up fights. Lunchtime staff should never restrain pupils without having learned how to do so and many education authorities offer specialist training in this area. You may have strong opinions about this subject and, if unclear, seek clarification and up-to-date information from your line manager.

Allegations made against staff

LTSs should discuss with their line manager any difficulties or a problem that may affect their relationship with particular children and accurate and comprehensive records must be maintained wherever concerns are raised about the conduct or actions of adults working with children and young people (DCSF 2007).

If you are the subject of allegations, you are advised to contact your union, or professional association. School will be expected to follow clear procedures for investigating allegations, and to provide guidance for all members of staff on what to do if they have concerns about the behaviour of their colleagues.

Every Child Matters and safeguarding children

The table below looks at the lunchtime supervisor's role in supporting the five *ECM* outcomes when safeguarding children.

ECM outcomes	The lunchtime supervisor's role in supporting the five ECM outcomes when safeguarding children
Be healthy	Develop children's social and emotional intelligence to engender self-respect and positive self-esteem
	Develop positive relationships and listen carefully to children
	Encourage children to talk about their feelings/circumstances
	Reassure children about their right to be safe and happy
	Develop an open and respectful lunchtime ethos
Stay safe	Recognise when children are displaying signs of distress
	Be aware of signs and symptoms of child abuse
	Listen carefully and do not judge what you hear
	Follow safeguarding children policy if you have concerns about a child
	Inform children about who you will need to pass information on to
	Never promise to keep secrets
	Share information with colleagues on a need to know basis
	Follow guidelines on appropriate physical conduct and restraint
	Record all incidents in line with school procedure
	Display zero tolerance towards bullying and violence or antisocial behaviour
Enjoy and achieve	Empower children to express themselves with confidence and to say what they want from others
	Encourage children to have respect for their own and other people's bodies
	Help children to understand their right to be safe
	Provide a positive and happy school lunchtime
Make a positive contribution	Ensure pupils are regularly consulted and offer feedback on issues that affect their lives.
	Encourage children to take responsibility for their own behaviour and to be supportive to others
	Help children to problem solve, and tackle difficulties assertively
	Encourage children to reflect on and take responsibility for their actions and to challenge others when necessary
Achieve economic wellbeing	Encourage children to be assertive and empowered citizens.

Conclusion

It is essential that all school staff keep an open mind, listen carefully to children, follow school policies and procedures and work together to protect the children in their care.

Further guidance and information

The Education Act 2002 and the Children Act 2004 outline the duty on local authorities to improve the wellbeing, and safeguard and promote the welfare, of children.

DCSF (2006) *Safeguarding Children and Safer Recruitment in Education.*

DCSF (2008) Staying Safe action plan.

Every Child Matters (www.everychildmatters.gov.uk)

Education and Inspections Act 2006

DCSF (2007) *Guidance for Safer Working Practice for Adults who Work with Children and Young People.*

Laming (2009) *The Protection of Children in England: A Progress Report* (TSO Publishing).

London Child Protection procedures, 3rd edition (2007).

The NSPCC website (http://www.nspcc.org.uk) offers a range of user-friendly fact sheets, pamphlets and other information.

Teachernet (www.teachernet.co.uk) – physical contact.

The Vetting and Barring Scheme (VBS). *Every Child Matters* website (http://www.everychildmatters.gov.uk/independentsafeguardingauthority/).

What to Do if You are Worried that a Child Is Being Abused (www.everychildmatters.gov.uk and www.teachernet.gov.uk/publications or DCSF Publications, Tel: 0845 60 222 60).

LTS training and career development

After many years of being given a low priority, training for support staff is now being developed. This is partly in response to the Workforce Agreement which aims to reduce teachers' workloads. The benefits of well trained and skilled support staff are considerable, and in September 2005 the TDA (the Training and Development Agency for schools) took on the role of working with schools to help them to develop and train their whole school workforce including support staff. The TDA in partnership with the School Workforce Development Board (SWDB) introduced a three-year national skills strategy 2006–2009, to ensure staff are trained, valued and have job satisfaction. The three main objectives were to: help schools to develop their workforce; create a framework of standards and qualifications; and to extend training opportunites to develop support staff.

Despite the recent improvements lunchtime staff in some schools describe the need for greater training opportunities. The *TES* outlines the findings of a UNISON report by Bruni de la Motte, *Time to Train* (2009), which states that about half of school support staff find it difficult to access training and only 40–50 per cent of support staff have had an annual review. It concludes: 'UNISON says too many schools fail to offer time, support or pay and that training for school support staff is inadequate in too many areas and needs to be addressed as a "matter of urgency".'

A new body, the Schools Support Staff Negotiating Body (SSSNB), came into being on 1 October 2008 to set pay and conditions for school support staff in English schools. They are in the process of negotiating new pay and conditions frameworks.

Payment for attending training

Support staff should be paid for all training that they are required to attend, as stated in note 22 of *Raising Standards and Tackling Workload: Implementing the National Agreement* July 2008). Managers will need to decide on a budget for LTS training, which includes overtime payment for part-time staff. If the training is longer than a half-day, cover for lunchtime duties will need to be organised.

Appraisal and professional development reviews

Your school may have gained Investors In People status, and so will be required to plan for the continuous professional development of *all* staff, not just teachers. TAs should be familiar with the appraisal system and many schools have introduced similar reviews for all LTSs to help focus on their own needs and development. This may be a formal appraisal or a less formal professional development discussion.

Continuing professional development (CPD) and career progression

Not all LTSs wish to be involved in extensive internal or external training. Many LTSs are busy people with strong family commitments or other jobs. You may not have time to think about career developments or to consider gaining further qualifications. We are now in a climate of lifelong learning in which people are encouraged to return to study at any stage of their life to gain skills and confidence to progress. You may have unhappy memories of your own school days, and returning to learning can be scary, especially if you haven't studied for a long time. Hopefully, with appropriate support, your confidence will grow.

Professional development portfolio

School staff are encouraged to keep records of their training and professional development in the form of a portfolio. This can be built on over the years to demonstrate training achievements and target future areas for development.

The TDA outlines how your portfolio may include:

- A title page
- A job description
- Personal achievements and positive comments to recognise achievement
- Training and professional development undertaken and evaluation of it
- Annual personal targets
- Any observation reports, performance management or development reviews
- Training log (details of CPD activities the person has undertaken)
- Performance evidence (e.g. annotated photographs, certificates, details of how the person had contributed to the life of the school)
- Membership of any working parties, or schemes.

Visit http://www.tda.gov.uk/teachers/continuingprofessionaldevelopment/cpd for further information.

Induction training

In *Unlock the Potential of Your Support Staff* (DCSF 2008), the TDA recommends that newly recruited support staff should have a pre-start visit with full introduction to their team and the school layout. They should also be offered an induction programme and a welcome pack plus a chance to clarify their role using a job description.

For many years the government has been offering teaching assistants an induction programme. In September 2003, the DfES developed introductory training for other support staff in schools. This was usually run in professional development centres and aimed to provide support staff with the chance meet together to learn about a range of work-related topics. For further information on induction, visit the TDA website (www.tda.gov.uk).

In-house training

Hopefully, you will be offered relevant school-based courses and INSET training on a regular basis. This is discussed in detail in previous chapters and in the Notes for Managers.

Courses run by your local education authority

Attending courses outside your school can offer the opportunity to share ideas and good practice with others. Courses for support staff will vary depending on where you work. Find out how training is advertised so that you can keep up to date.

Basic maths, English and computer skills

There is a growing number of options available to discuss with your line manager or training mentor (if there is one in post). To improve your basics mathematics, English or computing skills, many local colleges offer level 1 and level 2 courses in numeracy, literacy and information and computer technology (ICT). These may involve attending a number of sessions at a college where you can do trial tests, and gain individual and/or group support. If you prefer, work can be done independently on-line. To find out more, phone your local college or visit the Move On website (www.move-on.org.uk). This website offers free skills checks, brush-up courses and a list of local centres where you can register for courses. Your school may also be able to organise teaching sessions for groups of staff at your workplace. The DCSF Skills for Life Planner outlines opportunities for developing literacy, language and numeracy skills for school support staff. They also provide a DVD containing two films about training and development opportunities. For more information visit www.tda.gov.uk/sflplanner

UNISON training

UNISON, with the support of the TDA, has developed a training website covering current and developing roles within all types of schools. It is designed to help support staff and identify the training they need for different roles in schools. For further information visit www.skills4schools.org.uk

The National Occupational Standards

In June 2007, the final version of The National Occupational Standards (NOS) for support staff were published. These describe what a person needs to do, know and understand in their role. They are laid out in units, and describe key activities undertaken by the jobholder. They are written as benchmarks against which to access existing levels of knowledge and skills. There are NOS for staff who support teaching and learning in schools including for teaching assistants and higher level teaching assistants. There are also NOS for other support staff roles. The TDA has developed online NOS guidance to help staff to use the standards for a range of purposes including skills reviews, job descriptions and training and development (http://www.tda.gov.uk/support/NOS.aspx).

The Careers Development Framework for School Support Staff

There are a range of options available. Some LTSs may choose to obtain qualifications to apply for a teaching assistant post; others may wish to move into a welfare or play worker role, or become a parent support adviser or a qualified first aider. With workforce remodelling there may be a range of administrative responsibilities they can undertake. The Careers Development Framework for School Support Staff provides a list of national training and qualifications and also has a section on funding training. To find out more visit http://www.tda.gov.uk

Accredited qualifications for support staff

You can obtain a full list of accredited qualifications for support staff from the TDA website. There are a number of relevant Vocational Qualifications (VQs), National Vocational Qualifications (NVQs) or Scottish Vocational Qualifications (SVQs), which involve demonstrating that you are achieving a particular level of competence in the work you are doing.

Support work in schools

Since September 2004, an Award/Certificate for Support Work in Schools has been offered all over the country. This is a level 2 and 3 accredited qualification with a deliberately flexible structure to allow schools and candidates to select units to match their specific jobs. The sessions are usually school based to help participants to feel more comfortable in their surroundings. Once you have achieved this qualification you may choose to build on your learning to gain the equivalent of a level 2 NVQ.

Further training for teaching assistants

As TAs who also undertake lunchtime duty, you are likely to have completed a range of training concerning curriculum support and behaviour management in class, and have the advantage of observing and working closely with teaching staff. You may also be familiar with supervising playtime. TAs describe very different challenges experienced at lunchtime and many benefit from training specific to managing the midday break. This can be explored during appraisal and details have been provided throughout this book. As part of your CPD, you may wish to undertake VQs, NVQs, the Higher Level Teaching Assistant Award or a foundation degree.

The HLTA Award

You may also request to be put forward to undertake the Higher Level Teaching Assistant award (www.hlta.gov.uk).

You may find the UNISON Publication *School Remodelling: A UNISON Survival Guide* useful reading (www.tda.gov.uk/upload/resources/pdf/c/career_support_staff.pdf).

Foundation degree for support staff

As outlined in *A Foundation Degree Framework for the Children's Workforce* (TDA 2008):

Foundation degrees are designed to be accessible to all adult learners and the delivery mechanisms are flexible. They may be taken on a full- or part-time basis, and typically take two years full-time (two to four years part-time) to complete. Foundation degrees provide the learner with the opportunity to apply in the workplace the skills and knowledge learnt, as well as providing opportunities for applying learning from the workplace to academic learning.

For more information visit http://www.tda.gov.uk/upload/resources/pdf/f/fdf_final.pdf

Further information and useful contacts

Bruni de la Motte (2009) *Time to Train.* UNISON Education Publications.

DCSF (2007) *Deployment and Impact of Support Staff in Schools.*

DCSF (2008) *Unlock the Potential of Your Support Staff.* London: Department for Children, Schools and Families.

Foundation degree for support staff
(www.tda.gov.uk/upload/resources/pdf/f/fdf_final.pdf).

The HLTA Award – for details visit www.hlta.gov.uk

Learndirect advice service for people over 20 who have fewer than five GCSEs or an NVQ level 2. (www.learndirect-advice.co.uk or tel. 0800 100 900).

Learning and Skills Council – possible funding and advice for training (www.lsc.gov.uk/selectlsc.asp).

Move On website (www.move-on.org.uk).

Local Government Employers (2008) *Raising Standards and Tackling Workload: Implementing the National Agreement.*

The Schools Support Staff Negotiating Body (SSSNB) – came into being on 1 October 2008 to set pay and conditions for school support staff in England's schools. (http://www.teachernet.gov.uk).

Skills4Schools (www.skills4schools.org.uk or telephone 020 7551 1154).

Training and Development Agency (TDA) (www.tda.gov.uk or tel. 0845 6060 323).

PART 2

Notes for managers

Introduction

This part of the book is written for managers within the school, particularly those who line-manage LTSs or oversee the lunchtime break. Each section below should be read in conjunction with the relevant chapter in Part 1. Further reading and useful information is included at the end of each chapter.

There is a large amount of information in this book – more than most managers or LTSs will be able to retain in their day-to-day work. Consequently, you may wish to consider drawing up a set of 'simple rules' with LTSs. This involves describing in very succinct and memorable sentences how they are to undertake their duties. The beauty of simple rules is that they provide a clear framework for doing the job. The best ones are short, and few in number. For example:

- Always be child-centred
- Plan for good behaviour
- Keep everyone safe
- Consult the children
- Seek help when necessary.

Chapter 1 – The role of the LTS

Chapter 1 offers an overview of roles and responsibilities. The issues of accountability and confidentiality within the school community are also discussed. The chapter ends by focusing on the importance of lunchtime staff being valued by the school community. The activities can be used to ensure that LTSs are clear about their role and the expectations of others.

Who supervises at lunchtime?

For lunchtime to run smoothly, schools will need an adequately staffed and well managed team of LTSs. There are no nationally agreed guidelines stating the number of LTSs to be employed by each school, and some head teachers decide to fund an LTS for every class in the school, believing that the advantages outweigh the financial pressures. Others employ teaching assistants and play workers or a mixture of teaching assistants and LTSs to supervise lunchtimes, as a way to improve efficiency.

Using teaching assistants to supervise lunchtime

The number of support staff employed by schools has increased dramatically in recent years, which enables schools far greater flexibility when deciding how best to organise lunchtime.

Some schools prefer to employ LTSs specifically for the lunchtime period, which with appropriate support and training can prove to provide a high-quality lunchtime experience. This decision will be affected by a range of factors including that the calibre of lunchtime staff schools are able to recruit, teaching assistants' availability and willingness to undertake lunchtime duties and teaching staff's attitude towards releasing TAs from the classroom. If you have decided to use TAs to supervise all or part of lunchtime, consider the following. The whole school community will need to agree that:

- The school lunchtime would benefit from TA involvement
- This is an appropriate use of their time
- Teaching assistants who cover lunchtime will need time to sort out lunchtime issues and have a lunchtime break before returning to class
- They may also require time to attend lunchtime meetings when necessary
- Teaching staff can be flexible about TAs time away from the classroom
- The benefits of this arrangement outweigh the disadvantages.

When using a team with a mixture of TAs and non-TAs, managers will need to:

- Plan carefully to avoid creating a hierarchy of skill and knowledge
- Ensure all team members pull their weight and are allocated tasks according to their ability
- Set up excellent communication systems for all lunchtime staff
- Consider ways to help all staff feel valued (see Chapters 1 and 2)
- Ensure that channels of management and accountability are clear
- Ensure that contracts and job descriptions appropriately and accurately reflect the differences in responsibilities and line management when in class and when undertaking lunchtime duties, and that pay structures also reflect any differences if necessary
- Offer a lunchtime team meeting to openly explore working together
- Help TAs who work with children on an individual basis in class to enable them to allow the children greater independence at lunchtime
- Enable staff to share relevant information, skills and strategies
- Ensure all LTSs, including TAs, have appropriate specialised training in lunchtime issues where required
- Offer all staff appropriate support, performance management, training and career development (see Appendix).

Clarifying roles and responsibilities

To help clarify their role and responsibilities, all LTSs will need access to high-quality induction training including:

- User friendly summaries of school policies in relation to behaviour, health and safety, child protection, food, bullying, inclusion, confidentiality and physical contact. Meeting time may be required to help team members understand how these policies apply to them in practice. One head teacher described how he draws up specific, bullet-pointed summaries of relevant policies to help with this process
- An up-to-date job description

- An induction pack or notes outlining expectations. In some schools this is prepared by the senior LTSs and in others by the line manager
- Regular discussions with their line manager to reinforce good practice and to clarify issues of responsibility, accountability and confidentiality (see Chapters 1 and 2).

Accountability and confidentiality

LTSs will benefit from clear channels of accountability. This is discussed on pages 9–10 of Chapter 1 and activity is aimed to help develop thinking in this area.

Confidentiality is discussed in detail in Chapter 1, pages 12–13. The Activity on page 13 helps you and your LTS team explore this subject further. Managers may need to help LTSs to decide how best to respond to parents' 'everyday' enquiries about their children's eating and behaviour, and when to refer the parent to teaching staff for further discussion. See page 13 for a brief discussion.

Managers regularly have to decide how much information to share with LTSs about the children they work with. It can be difficult to find the right balance between providing sufficient information to enable LTSs to work well, while also respecting the child's right to confidentiality. TAs who undertake lunchtime duty may have far greater knowledge about the children and will need to know how much to share with their non-TA colleagues.

The role of the senior LTS

Schools will need to decide whether to appoint a senior LTS. A strong senior LTS can enhance team effectiveness, improve communication and staff morale, and consequently make your job easier. Difficulties arise, however, when an unsuitable person has been appointed, often on the basis of long-service as an LTS, rather than the potential to fulfil a supervisory role. Some schools appoint an HLTA for this role and accountability may need to be clarified (see case study in Chapter 1, page 10). Many schools under-use the senior LTS and fail to fully recognise their management potential. Senior LTSs often benefit from further training in basic management skills.

Valuing lunchtime supervisors

As with the pupils, the way LTSs are treated within the school will have an effect on their self-esteem and confidence. On a whole school, systemic level, the way that support staff are treated is an important indication of how your institution values its least powerful members. To be an effective role model, managers *will* develop relationships with LTSs in a way that demonstrates how you would like *them* to relate to the children.

Chapter 1 describes how LTSs can gain the respect of other staff and children by behaving in an accountable and professional manner.

Schools can reinforce their status and authority by:

- Ensuring that the school community are clear about the LTSs role and responsibilities. See Chapter 1, Activities 1 and 3 (pages 8 and 10)
- Creating systems to remind children and parents of authority and the importance of the LTS role
- Having expectations that all staff will treat LTSs with respect, regardless of whether children are present
- Encouraging LTSs to use the staffroom
- Considering how LTSs are to be referred to – are they known as the dinner ladies, even if this isn't their job? Are they called by their first names when other staff are referred to by Mr or Mrs, followed by their surnames?
- Putting pictures of all staff, including the LTSs on display in the school reception area

- Including LTSs in school events (e.g. by inviting them to school concerts, outings or staff social events) (see examples of bad practice, Chapter 2, page 15)
- Linking particular LTSs with particular classes or year groups to improve their relationships and status
- Providing LTSs with appropriate guidance communication and training
- Offering LTSs the opportunity to develop skills to work in other roles and capacities within the school in line with workforce remodelling
- Paying LTSs overtime to attend relevant meetings and training (as stated in note 22 of *Raising Standards and Tackling Workload: Implementing the National Agreement*, July 2008).

Also see *Using Teaching Assistants to Supervise Lunchtime*, outlined on page 128 of Notes for managers.

Chapter 2 – Communication within the school

Chapter 2 considers how schools can create and implement tailor-made systems to ensure a two-way structured exchange of information.

Information about the school – a checklist

Are there systems in place to ensure the following:	Yes	No
Are LTSs receiving an induction pack containing up to date policies and procedure	☐	☐
All LTSs receive the school newsletter and other relevant letters, lists and minutes	☐	☐
Information is regularly updated?	☐	☐
LTSs are informed about staff changes and how they are introduced to new staff members	☐	☐
LTSs are informed about changes in school rules and routines	☐	☐
Communication is timed appropriately to avoid LTSs learning about changes from the children	☐	☐
LTSs are informed about school events including fundraising initiatives, special assemblies, staff outings and lunches	☐	☐
That LTSs have forums to feedback their ideas and concerns.	☐	☐

Information about the children

The amount of information and detail shared about the children with LTSs is likely to be decided on a need to know basis and appropriate confidentiality will be at the forefront of managers' thinking. LTSs often feel they are given insufficient amounts of information about the children to do their job effectively. TAs who undertake lunchtime duty will often know more about the children they work with.

Are LTSs provided with the following:	Yes	No
A list of children's special medical needs, displayed in a confidential place	☐	☐
An up-to-date list of children's special dietary requirements, or eating issues placed in an appropriately accessible, confidential place	☐	☐
Sufficient details about children's special educational needs. This may be discussed in meetings with other staff members or communicated in writing	☐	☐
Information about children who are bullying or being bullied	☐	☐

	Yes	No
Strategies for managing children with particularly challenging behaviour. Again this may involve discussion with other staff members including the SENCO	☐	☐
Information about circumstances that may be affecting children including family problems	☐	☐
Systems to ensure that LTSs can pass to the appropriate people information about children's behaviour and wellbeing.	☐	☐

Meetings

Meetings are a crucial means of communication. They can, however, be time-consuming and costly. Chapter 2 explores what types of meetings can be beneficial and how frequent they should be. Some schools require their lunchtime staff to attend meetings in their own time.

Research by the DCSF – *Deployment and Impact of Support Staff in Schools* (July 2007) – states that in the previous year, only a half of support staff were paid for extra hours worked. *In Raising Standards and Tackling Workload: Implementing the National Agreement* (July 2008), local government employers concludes that: 'There is some evidence that on occasions, support staff with established contractual arrangements are being expected to undertake "unpaid overtime". This is unacceptable.'

Meetings checklist

Do you offer LTSs meetings...	Yes	No
With the head teacher or another delegated line manager on a regular basis?	☐	☐
With the class teacher if relevant?	☐	☐
With the SENCO to discuss specific pupils special educational needs and behaviour?	☐	☐
With key stage teams?	☐	☐
With the peer group (comprising the LTS and the senior LTS without senior managers being present)?	☐	☐
With the senior LTS on a regular basis and expect her/him to liaise with her team?	☐	☐
With the whole team on a regular basis?	☐	☐
To allow sufficient time for issues to be discussed?	☐	☐
To value your LTSs by paying them overtime to attend meetings?	☐	☐
To encourage LTSs to share the responsibility for organising and contributing to meetings?	☐	☐
To encourage LTSs to voice their opinion as well as using the time to share information?	☐	☐
To invite LTSs to attend relevant whole staff INSET days?	☐	☐

Written communication

Providing adequate written communication is an effective way to ensure that information is shared. Bear in mind that the literacy and ICT skills within the team are likely to vary.

Do all LTSs have access to the following:	Yes	No
Regularly distributed and updated communication that it is written in simple, jargon-free language	☐	☐

	Yes	No
The school newsletter	☐	☐
Lists of dates of school terms, INSET days and other important staff events	☐	☐
Minutes from relevant meetings (or parts of meetings)	☐	☐
A message or briefing book providing information by teaching staff about children's needs or difficulties	☐	☐
Lists of children's medical needs, allergies and dietary needs	☐	☐
A daily staff briefing, if appropriate	☐	☐
An up-to-date list of children attending lunchtime clubs, outings and any other relevant activities	☐	☐
The detention book	☐	☐
Forms, slips or books used to pass information between LTSs and other staff including the office staff and the site manager/caretaker	☐	☐
Copies of relevant guidelines, policies and procedures, possibly in summary form	☐	☐
Written communication placed in an accessible location	☐	☐
Their own noticeboard, pigeon-hole or message book	☐	☐
The school Managed Learning Environment (MLE).	☐	☐

Managed learning environment as a forum for communication

Schools may wish to set up a virtual lunchtime room on the MLE specifically for lunchtime information and communication. LTSs will need training and support to access this as well as adequate time to check in on a daily basis. For more information visit http://publications.teachernet.gov.uk/default.aspx?PageFunction=productdetails&PageMode=publications&ProductId=15003&

The handover of information before and after the lunchtime

A two-way structured exchange of information before and after the lunchtime will help to ensure that relevant facts are shared and acted upon. Children will consequently view the lunchtime as a consistent part of the school day. See Chapter 2, page 21 for a full discussion.

Feedback following serious incidents

Following serious lunchtime incidents, LTSs need to know what happened and how the children were dealt with. Such feedback can alleviate the regularly voiced concern that not enough is being done. Managers can also encourage LTSs to ask for information rather than to wait passively for it.

A staff debrief

LTSs often benefit from the opportunity to meet together informally for a few minutes at the end of lunchtime to share experiences and discuss incidents. This offers peer support and can help to reduce stress. TAs who undertake lunchtime duty often feel pressured to return to the classroom (see Case Study 2 in Chapter 1, page 12).

Chapter 3 – Building relationships with children

Most senior managers and head teachers are aware of the value of employing LTSs who can effectively interact with children. TAs who also supervise lunchtime have an obvious advantage in this area. This chapter outlines a range of skills and practices to help LTSs to develop positive relationships with the children they supervise. The activities can be used to encourage the acquisition of skills in areas including being child-centred, encouraging, being a good listener and an effective communicator. The chapter concludes by exploring factors that interfere with positive relationships and how to overcome these hurdles.

Developing LTSs' understanding of the factors that affect children's lives

Enabling support staff to understand the issues affecting children's lives can help them to relate to children with greater sensitivity. This can be achieved by inviting them to special school celebrations, assemblies and training sessions.

Organisational issues

The Primary National Strategy document *Playtimes and Lunchtimes* (DfES2005a) describes developing 'systems to link particular lunchtime staff with particular classes or year groups, so they are part of the class or year group team'. This has obvious advantages when it comes to developing relationships with children and creating a sense of belonging for LTSs. Managers will need to help LTSs to avoid over-identifying with their class or group at the expense of the other children.

The chance to observe good practice

LTSs who are not also teaching assistants may not have many opportunities to observe skilled teaching staff interacting with children in the playground or classroom. Some schools believe the benefits of such observation are so great that they pay their LTSs to work in the classroom for a limited period. It will help if teachers or managers can engage in regular discussions to explain how they sustain relationships with the most challenging children. Pairing an inexperienced LTS with a more experienced member of the LTS team can also be helpful.

Chapters 4 and 5 – Managing behaviour at lunchtime

Chapter 4 examines strategies and whole school practices that can be developed to encourage positive behaviour at lunchtime. It also explores some of the underlying reasons for children's misbehaviour and outlines a number of theories that have influenced behaviour management in schools. The activities, the checklists and the behaviour management case studies on pages 39–40 can be used in training sessions.

Chapter 5 explores a whole school model of behaviour management and effective strategies to deal with and challenge unacceptable behaviour. The chapter concludes by focusing on challenges including verbal abuse and violence. There are activities including a number of discussions and case studies to be used to develop staff knowledge and skills.

Developments

Safe to Learn: Embedding Anti-bullying in Schools (DCSF 2007) outlines how:

> The Education and Inspection Act 2006 requires that head teachers *must* determine measures on behaviour and discipline that form the school's behaviour policy, acting in accordance with the governing body's statement of principles in so doing. Measures, in this context, include rules, rewards, sanctions and behaviour-management strategies. The policy determined by the head teacher must include measures to be taken with a view to 'encouraging good behaviour and respect for others on the part of pupils and, in particular, preventing all forms of bullying among pupils'.
>
> The law empowers head teachers, to such extent as is reasonable, to regulate the behaviour of pupils when they are off school site (which is particularly pertinent to regulating cyberbullying) and empowers members of school staff to impose disciplinary penalties for inappropriate behaviour.

The Education and Inspection Act 2006 outlines how all teachers and other staff in charge of pupils have the power to discipline, but the head teacher may limit the power to apply particular sanctions to certain staff. This needs to be made clear in relation to lunchtime staff.

Whole school practice

Lunchtime is likely to be most successful when LTSs are consistently working alongside other staff members to manage children's behaviour. Schools, on the other hand, must agree on clear and consistent rules and routines so that all staff members 'sing from the same song sheet'. This requires regular whole school discussion, feedback and review of practice. Chapters 4 and 5 explore how to achieve a high standard of behaviour management at lunchtime. Schools will need to:

- Have an adequately staffed and well managed team of LTSs
- Use INSET days, training sessions and meetings to focus on consistently implemented behaviour management strategies and policies
- Make the behaviour policy accessible and understandable to LTSs
- Encourage LTSs to be assertive, proactive and to plan for children's good behaviour at lunchtime (see Chapter 5, pages 40–43)
- Ensure that LTSs use a range of strategies to encourage positive behaviour (see Chapter 4, pages 40–45)
- Encourage LTSs to develop positive relationships with children and to manage behaviour in a way that minimises confrontation (see Chapters 3, 4 and 5, pages 50–53)
- Agree what constitutes unacceptable behaviour and ensure that the consequences are clear and that sanctions are consistently implemented
- Share relevant information about the children on an ongoing basis
- Offer support, training and senior management back-up to help LTSs cope with the most challenging behaviour
- Manage some of the physical and environmental issues that affect children's behaviour (see Chapter 4, page 45)
- Help LTSs to encourage children to take responsibility for their own behaviour (see Chapter 4, page 44)
- Provide an excellent role models for children and staff (see Notes for managers, page 129)

Ensure that the consequences of misbehaviour are clear and that sanctions and rewards are consistently implemented.

In school…	Yes	No
Is there an agreed range of rewards, consequences and sanctions for unacceptable lunchtime behaviour?	☐	☐
Are LTSs clear about their powers to use sanctions and helped to do so in a reasonable and consistent way (see list Chapter 5, page 48)?	☐	☐
Do LTSs have autonomy to distribute rewards during the lunchtime break?	☐	☐
Are systems in place to ensure that there is consistent practice during playtimes, lunchtimes and during other times of the day?	☐	☐
Is the LTSs' authority undermined by contradiction or intervention by other staff members?	☐	☐
Are 'time out' sanctions in place and used consistently?	☐	☐
Is there an indoor 'cool down' space (such as a detention room)?	☐	☐

	Yes	No
Are there systems to provide LTSs with feedback on the outcomes of more serious incidents?	☐	☐
Are systems regularly discussed and reviewed?	☐	☐

Offer special support, training and senior management back-up to help LTSs to cope with the most challenging behaviour

You can:

- Inform LTSs of suitable strategies and sanctions to be used with particular children (see discussion in Chapter 5, page 48)

- Clarify your expectations about LTSs' use of force to control or restrain pupils

  This will include discussions about what constitutes acceptable physical contact with pupils. It is advisable to have school procedures addressing these issues, including how LTSs are expected to break up fights, and provide specialist training, particularly if the LTSs are required to restrain pupils physically. For further information see Chapter 5, page 53

  The DCSF's 'The use of force to control or restrain pupils – non-statutory guidance for schools in England' has replaced the DfES circular 10/98. It discusses in detail Section 93 of the Education and Inspections Act 2006, which is highly relevant. Schools are advised to create their own policy on the use of reasonable force to control or restrain pupils and issues to consider include breaking up fights at lunchtime, see www.teachernet.gov.uk/_doc/12187/ACFD89B.pdf

- Implement special lunchtime arrangements, including: indoor provisions and extra support for troubled children or structured back-up systems for the LTSs. This has been explored in greater detail in Chapter 5

- Create systems to ensure there is back-up from senior managers in the playground or in the dining room when necessary (see discussion Chapter 5, page 53)

- Offer LTSs support when they have been hurt or seriously verbally abused by pupils (see discussion in Chapter 5, page 54)

- Encourage LTSs to explore ways to conduct themselves professionally, even when facing extremely provocative behaviour from pupils (see discussion Chapter 5, pages 48–9 and page 54)

Chapter 6 – Dealing with bullying

Chapter 6 explores the complexity of the problem of bullying including what constitutes bullying, who is likely to bully or be bullied, and the devastating consequences for the victims. It highlights the rise of cyber-bullying in primary school and looks at what schools can do to deal with these problems at lunchtime, both on a whole school and on an individual level.

Recent government initiatives are outlined in the Chapter.

Ofsted inspections

The 2006 Education Act introduced a new duty on schools to promote the wellbeing of their pupils, and following a consultation process from September 2009, the new Ofsted benchmarks for wellbeing will be introduced. This will include how safe pupils feel and whether the school effectively deals with bullying. Schools are required to consult with pupils regularly, and to incorporate the results of evaluation of their anti-bullying policy in their Ofsted self-evaluation form.

Offering LTSs appropriate anti-bullying training

Safe to Learn: Embedding Anti-bullying Work in Schools (DCSF 2007) outlines the need for regular review of training, specific staff induction and continuing professional development (CPD).

For a full list of relevant training topics for LTSs in this subject see Chapter 6. LTSs will also need to be aware of the school policy and procedures for dealing with bullying – see Chapter 6, pages 60–64. Finding relevant anti-bullying training can be difficult and the LEA may be able to provide input. There is a list of organisations offering support and training at the end of the *Safe to Learn* report.

To initiate further discussion, managers may wish to encourage LTSs to complete the bullying checklist included at the end of Chapter 6.

Schools are likely to recommend a range of strategies to identify and deal with bullying which can be adapted to fit the circumstances. The whole school community should be involved and progress should be monitored on a regular basis. This has been discussed in Chapter 6, page 61. LTSs will also need to know in which circumstances they are expected to deal with incidents of bullying themselves, and when, in more serious or persistent incidents, to pass details on to others to be dealt with.

Developing the playground

As discussed in Chapters 6 and 8, developing the playground can decrease the incidents of bullying.

A playground checklist for managers

Does the school...	Yes	No
Encourage children to be proactive in response to unacceptable behaviour?	☐	☐
Review playground supervision on a regular basis?	☐	☐
Ensure all areas of the playground are supervised, especially areas that are hard to see?	☐	☐
Have clear procedures for supervising the toilets when necessary?	☐	☐
Train supervisors to recognise and respond to bullying?	☐	☐
Ensure that boredom is kept to a minimum by providing equipment or structured activities?	☐	☐
Zone the playground to decrease marginalisation or isolation of children?	☐	☐
Introduce playground initiatives to create an anti-bullying ethos?	☐	☐

Developing anti-bullying playground initiatives

There are a number of useful case studies on www.teachernet.gov.uk and in Anti-bullying guidance for schools (http://www.healthyschools.gov.uk).

Chapter 7 – Healthy eating

Chapter 7 discusses the introduction of new school food and nutrient-based standards, and a range of initiatives to improve the dining room environment. It briefly outlines what we should be eating to remain healthy and the serious problems that can result from an unhealthy diet. The role of the LTS is explored in relation to encouraging healthy eating, helping children to develop socially at lunchtime, creating a positive dining room environment, monitoring children's food intake, teaching pupils about food and participating in whole school food initiatives. The chapter discusses the food-related emotional problems experienced by a small number of primary age children.

Who is responsible for school food and drinks?

The responsibility for the provision of school meals lies with the local authorities, or directly with the schools if the local authority has delegated the school meals budget. This includes ensuring that the food meets the standards for food provision 'other than lunch' and the food and nutrient-based standards for lunch. There is a voluntary code of practice for drinks provided in schools. For more information visit the School Food Trust website (www.schoolfoodtrust.org.uk). For details on the role of the governors, see the Food Standards Agency and the National Governors' Council's strategic policy framework for governing bodies on the School Food Trust website: *Food Policy in Schools: A Strategic Policy Framework for Governing Bodies* (revised September 2007).

The Healthy Schools programme

This is a joint Department of Health and Department for Children, Schools and Family (DCSF) initiative. For more details see the criteria for healthy schools 'A Guide for Schools' (www.wiredforhealth.gov.uk/cat.php?catid=851).

Creating a whole school food policy

To obtain Healthy School status, schools are required to have a whole school food policy that includes packed lunch guidelines. These should be reviewed every two years and enable the school community to have a shared philosophy on all aspects of food. You can obtain guidance on how to set a whole school food policy from:

- The School Food Trust
- The British Nutrition Foundation, which gives a detailed eight-step programme on developing and implementing a whole school food policy, including a sample guide and a sample policy
- The DCSF which has funded a training programme and a Food in School Toolkit (http://www.foodinschools.org/fis_toolkit.php)
- The healthy school co-ordinator in your area
- The School Food Trust helpline (0800 0895 001).

School food groups or school nutrition action groups

The government strongly recommend the setting up of School Food Groups or School Nutrition Action Groups with the aims of developing healthy food initiatives and a positive school meal experience. Membership can include a governor, a senior manager, a school council representative, a parent, a member from the catering staff and an LTS. The group may also include a healthy school or nutritional adviser. Improvements should be included in the school development plans and policies.

The School Food Trust school food checklist

This on-line interactive tool has been developed to assist schools to check whether their lunch provision is compliant with the food-based standards for school lunches and other school food provision. Visit http://schoolfoodchecklist.schoolfoodtrust.org.uk

Ofsted inspections

Since September 2005, Ofsted has systematically reviewed the quality of school meals as part of regular school inspections. They also perform detailed inspections of the nutritional content of school food in a sample of schools in every local authority. From September 2009, Ofsted will be looking for evidence from all schools on a set of wellbeing benchmarks. These include how the school promotes healthy eating and the percentage of pupils who eat school dinners.

Improving the eating environment

A great deal has been written about the benefits of a positive eating environment and many schools have made considerable improvements in this area. A range of initiatives is outlined in the government's guidelines *A Fresh Look at the School Meal Experience* (June 2007), obtainable on the School Food Trust website. There are large numbers of useful case studies on this website and on Teachernet (www.teachernet.gov.uk/).

Funding for healthy activities linked to school food

Schools often initiate their own whole school healthy eating fundraising activities. As well as the Standards Fund Grant, there is a range of school grants available to apply for. Further details are available in the funding section of the School Food Trust (www.school foodtrust.org.uk).

Initiatives to encourage healthy eating and the uptake of school dinners

The government has made considerable efforts to encourage the uptake of healthier school dinners. There is some concern that the increased cost of healthy ingredients is making school meals too expensive, particularly in times of recession. In October 2007, The School Food Trust launched a campaign to increase the number of children eating school food by one million per day by 2010. For more information visit www.schoolfoodtrust.org.uk/ millionmeals

Recent initiatives

In *Healthy Lives, Brighter Futures: The Strategy for Children and Young People's Health* (Feburary 2009), the government outlined how it will: 'initiate pilots, testing the health and educational outcomes we could expect from introducing free school meals for all primary pupils'. It also commits to consulting on changing the law to enable schools to subsidise school meals.

Packed lunch initiatives

As part of the whole school policy, schools have produced guidelines, information and sample menus for healthier packed lunches. There are useful links on the School Food Trust website under *Packed Lunch Links*.

Consulting parents, children and catering staff

Children should be consulted on a regular basis and many schools have sought regular feedback from pupils about their attitude towards food options and dining room initiatives by using questionnaires and pupil discussion groups. Parents may have strong opinions about what their children eat and will need to be consulted about major changes and developments. *Jamie's School Dinners* attracted hostility from both children and parents. Removing items of food from children's lunchboxes can generate strong responses. Schools use a range of methods to communicate with parents including: newsletters/leaflets/letters about school food, sending home sample menus, parents' evenings, information on the school website and taster sessions. In more than half the primary schools recently surveyed, parents were invited to eat in school. Meetings with catering staff have found to be extremely productive and of those surveyed 89% of primary schools reported that they involved catering staff in enforcing school food policy (The School Food Trust 2007).

Consulting head teachers – The School Food Panel – survey of head teachers

The School Food panel is comprised of representatives from approximately 400 schools. Each term, head teachers are asked to complete a questionnaire on current food-related issues. For further information visit
http://www.schoolfoodtrust.org.uk/doc_item.asp? DocCatId= 1&DocId=42

The role of the LTS

The School Food Panel: Fourth Survey of Head Teachers (spring 2008) focuses on lunchtime staffing and lunchtime arrangements. The research shows that although managing behaviour, the environment and the dinner queue were seen by heads to be their most important function, 88 per cent of head teachers believed that encouraging children to try new foods, and 62 per cent said education of children about healthier eating, were also a significant part of the LTS's role. Lunchtime staff were found to be involved in school discussion groups in just under half of primary schools surveyed. Visit: http://www.schoolfoodtrust.org.uk/UploadDocs/Library/Documents/sft_sfp4_report_nov08.pdf

In Chapter 7, the ways LTSs can contribute to healthy eating have been outlined in detail.

Management checklist

Are your LTSs...	Yes	No
Aware of a whole school food policy and involved in its implementation?	☐	☐
Included in food discussion groups?	☐	☐
Encouraging children to eat healthy options without pressurising them?	☐	☐
Educating children about healthy options?	☐	☐
Rewarding healthy eating?	☐	☐
Clear about the food children can and cannot bring into school?	☐	☐
Aware of what to do if forbidden food is brought into school in lunchboxes?	☐	☐
Helping children to understand and be sensitive to foods from a range of cultures?	☐	☐
Clear about children's special dietary needs?	☐	☐
Meeting with managers, catering staff and other relevant people to agree on acceptable practice?	☐	☐
Encouraged to report back on any areas of difficulties in the dining room or in relation to food provisions?	☐	☐
Helped to cope with reluctant or faddy eaters?	☐	☐
Aware of how to respond to children experiencing problems with food?	☐	☐
Included in occasional school council meetings and other forums to elicit pupils' feedback?	☐	☐
Encouraged to use food-based activities during wet play and at other times (see details in Chapter 7)?	☐	☐
Invited to participate in whole school food initiatives at other times of the day?	☐	☐
Encouraged to use the internet at work to access relevant information?	☐	☐

You may also wish to complete the dining room checklist in the healthy eating chapter, page 74.

Healthy eating training and qualifications for LTSs and catering staff

Lunchtime staff differ greatly in their own knowledge and commitment to healthy eating. The authors of the School Food Panel's fourth survey of head teachers, November 2008, conclude that opportunities exist to further train and 'up skill and engage supervisory staff in the promotion of healthier eating'. This can include discussions with LTSs about how they talk to children to encourage them to eat and how they can be most effective. For more information about training courses available, contact your healthy school co-coordinator or visit the School Food Trust website http://www.schoolfoodtrust.org.uk/stacker_detail.asp? Contentid=304

Chapter 8 – Play at lunchtime

Chapter explores how the lunchtime break can offer children the chance to play constructively and to be active physically. When successful, this can occupy children and improve behaviour.

Government initiatives

In response to concerns about children's obesity levels and inactive lifestyles, the National Play Strategy (December 2008) outlines plans to improve and develop play facilities for children throughout the country. In response to concerns about the erosion of playtime available to children due to the shortening of lunchtime and playtime, the government acknowledges the need for further research into how schools can best organise breaks and lunchtimes so that pupils are able to play, 'and what pupils own views are on this in the context of schools promoting their wellbeing'.

Healthy Lives, Brighter Futures: The Strategy for Children and Young People's Health (February 2009) outlines how schools in partnership with other sport providers should strive to increase the amount of sporting activity for children aged 5 to 16 from two hours to five hours per week.

The Youth Sport Trust, in conjunction with Sainsbury's Active Kids, has developed the Top Activity Programme Partnership to target pupils who, traditionally, do not participate in sport. This offers training and a range of equipment and activities to be delivered either on school or community sites and led by a wide range of deliverers including lunchtime supervisors. Visit www.youthsporttrust.org/subpage/working-in-partnership-sainsburys/index.html for more information.

Inspecting play provision in schools

From September 2009, Ofsted will use new wellbeing benchmarks when inspecting schools. These will include the quality of play provision and the amount of structured play.

Chapter 8 also explores how to develop a positive playground ethos by having a well trained team of LTSs with the skills to facilitate play when necessary, and the wisdom to know when to leave children to their own devices. The provision of appropriate playground equipment and activities and the organisation of the playgrounds are discussed in some detail. The activities and the case studies included can be used to review existing practice and to develop inclusive play at lunchtime.

The role of the LTS

Lunchtime staff will vary greatly in their desire and ability to initiate, facilitate and participate in play. The number of LTSs in post is also likely to impact on their capacity to involve themselves, at the same time as keeping the children safe. Managers may consider recruiting play leaders and extra teaching assistants, as well as delegating play responsibilities to the more enthusiastic lunchtime supervisors (see Chapter 8, page 85). Although increasing the numbers of staff at lunchtime may be expensive, the benefits for behaviour and learning are considerable. Researchers such as Thomson and Blatchford outline a worrying trend for schools to adopt a 'constraining and interventionist' stance (see Chapter 8, page 83 and Chapter 10, page 102). These arguments make interesting reading and challenge much of the current thinking about playground development. Health and safety considerations are revisited in Chapter 10.

Training for LTSs

Facilitating children's play requires special skills, which differ considerably from those needed by LTSs in other areas of their work. This is discussed in Chapter 8, pages 84, 86 and 88.

Many lunchtime staff benefit from being taught how to set up, teach and sustain activities. It is easy to assume a level of skill that may not exist. The Guidelines for Keeping Lunchtime Activities Successful on page 86 may also prove helpful. Regular discussions to review activities are essential for success to be sustainable.

A list of relevant play work training has been provided on page 92.

Providing playground equipment and activities

This is discussed in detail in Chapter 8, page 85. The checklist below summarises many of the issues.

Does your school…	Yes	No
Build in time to plan for playground games and activities?	☐	☐
Offer a variety of playground equipment and activities?	☐	☐
Have equipment that is suitable for a range of children, including those with a disability?	☐	☐
Provide adequate and accessible storage space for playground equipment?	☐	☐
Have systems for maintaining, checking, distributing, collecting and replacing playground equipment?	☐	☐
Offer a range of activities to meet the needs of different pupils?	☐	☐
Ensure that football does not dominate the playground?	☐	☐
Offer initiatives to encourage children to take responsibility for caring for playground equipment?	☐	☐
Consult and actively involve pupils in relation to the available activities and equipment?	☐	☐
Rotate the playground equipment and activities to provide novelty value?	☐	☐
Equip lunchtime staff with the skills to teach and sustain activities?	☐	☐
Recruit play leaders or appropriate staff members to initiate games and activities?	☐	☐
Encourage buddies to play with the younger children?	☐	☐
Review playground activities on a regular basis with the lunchtime staff?	☐	☐
Budget and fundraise to finance the equipment?	☐	☐
Involve LTSs and parents in fundraising initiatives?	☐	☐

A playground organisation checklist

	Yes	No
Is the playground zoned to include an area for active play, quiet activities, sports and imaginative play?	☐	☐
Is the playground marked to encourage imaginative play?	☐	☐

	Yes	No
Are there netball or basketball hoops and other fixed equipment?	☐	☐
Are there seats, benches, dens and other interesting structures?	☐	☐
Does the playground have out of bounds areas and, if so, are they really necessary?	☐	☐
Is there fixed equipment such as climbing frames?	☐	☐
Is there a covered play area?	☐	☐
Does the playground have art to provide colour and texture?	☐	☐
Is there an adequate amount of trees or flowers?	☐	☐
Are there adequate water fountains, litter bins and shade?	☐	☐
Does playground zoning unnecessarily limit the children's freedom?	☐	☐
Would you spend time in your school grounds if you didn't have to?	☐	☐

Funding

Playground development can be expensive, although even without large amounts of money, a great deal can be accomplished by using imagination and initiative. Learning through Landscapes provides a detailed funding pack for its members, and information about other sources of funding can be found on page 92.

Resources

A list of resources about playgrounds and playground games is included at the end of Chapter 8.

Chapter 9 – Managing wet play

Chapter 9 covers planning, preparation, practical organisation of space and staff, and the creative use of resources and activities. Ideas for games, activities and the content of wet play boxes are also included.

Organising wet play

Consider the numbers of LTSs available to oversee wet play and how they can adequately cover supervision of the dining room and the classrooms (and/or other rooms occupied by the children). You may wish to employ relief staff during a wet play if this is practicable. You should assist the LTS to manage the existing space flexibly, and to accurately assess and manage the risk of wet play activities (see Chapter 10). Behaviour management can be particularly challenging during wet play and LTSs need to know how to access your support and back-up when necessary. Also see Chapters 4 and 5.

The checklist below will help managers to review existing practice and to plan for improvements.

A manager's wet play checklist

During wet play, do you...	Yes	No
Have clear systems to decide and communicate that it is wet play?	☐	☐
Have systems of communication between the teachers and the LTSs, clarifying what classroom equipment can be used?	☐	☐
Have adequate numbers of LTSs to supervise the classrooms and the dining room?	☐	☐

	Yes	No
Manage the available indoor space constructively?	☐	☐
Provide specific wet play equipment and imaginative activities to occupy the children?	☐	☐
Ensure that this equipment is suitable for the range of different pupils attending your school?	☐	☐
Undertake regular risk assessments of wet play equipment and activities?	☐	☐
Ensure that all lunchtime staff are clear about fire procedures including how to evacuate the building and activate the fire alarm?	☐	☐
Practise fire drill during lunchtime?	☐	☐
Have clear wet play rules and routines on display to be referred to?	☐	☐
Provide LTSs with guidance on how best to supervise children with behavioural difficulties or special educational needs?	☐	☐
Use older buddies to help with the younger classes?	☐	☐
Offer management back-up when necessary?	☐	☐
Build in planning and review time for your wet play activities?	☐	☐
Ask the children how they experience wet play and what could improve the experience?	☐	☐
Encourage LTSs to use their skills and talents to entertain the children constructively?	☐	☐
Provide wet play clubs?	☐	☐

Chapter 10 – Keeping children safe and healthy at lunchtime

Chapter 10 explores measures schools can take to keep children safe at lunchtime in the playground and inside the school building. Legal responsibilities are outlined, as well as the role of the LTS in assessing and managing risk, coping with accidents, administering first aid, recording incidents and dealing with pupils' special needs. The included activities encourage staff to review existing practice and to consider appropriate action to reduce and manage risk.

The school's responsibilities

The lunchtime period often creates considerable pressures and anxieties for managers. Large numbers of children are 'released' after a structured morning in class, and often non-teaching staff are required to keep them safe and happy.

For schools, the legal responsibilities for employers and employees under the 1974 Health and Safety at Work Act are outlined in the DfES Guidance 0803/2001 *Health and Safety: Responsibilities and Powers*. A comprehensive list of up-to-date and relevant health and safety guidelines and information can be obtained from the Teachernet website (www.teachernet.gov.uk/wholeschool/healthandsafety/responsibilities/visitsresponsibilities section4/).

The government's *Staying Safe Action Plan* (Feb 2008) also outlines a range of useful health and safety initiatives.

The health and safety policy

Under the same Act, employers must have a health and safety policy, and employees must be consulted and made aware of their roles and responsibilities as defined in it. LTSs are likely to require your support in accessing relevant parts of the policy.

Training for LTSs in health and safety matters

The employer is required by law to provide health and safety training to ensure that staff are competent to carry out their responsibilities.

Relevant training for LTSs could include:

- Risk assessment
- Initiating safe play
- Coping with accidents and emergencies at lunchtime
- Playground security
- First aid
- Fire procedures
- Recording and reporting incidents
- Working with children who have special medical needs.

All the above topics have been discussed in detail in Chapter 10. Some will be briefly discussed below.

Initiating safe play

This has been discussed in Chapter 10, page 102. LTSs may require assistance to find a balance between allowing children to play in a stimulating way, whilst keeping them safe. Although tempting, the risks of always erring on the side of caution and over-restricting children have their own set of problems.

Chris Lowe, *TES* Legal Editor, says:

> The risk to children during break time has always been there, and short of clear and gross negligence…the courts have striven to uphold the rights of children to learn from play. Health and safety laws do not require schools to ban everything remotely dangerous. Schools need to consider risk that is 'reasonably foreseeable' and to take 'reasonably practicable' steps to avoid or to minimise them.

(Northern, *TES* 2004)

Coping with accidents and emergencies at lunchtime

Accidents and emergencies will happen. Having clear roles, procedures and well prepared, competent staff can reduce their risk and the potential damage caused. The activity on page 105 encourages LTSs to anticipate and discuss in advance how best to respond to a range of accidents and emergencies.

Playground security

Details of the Working Group on School Security (WGSS) recommendations can be found on the Teachernet website. A DfES-commissioned research report, *School Security Concerns* (Lloyd and Ching 2003), makes interesting reading. There is also the DCSF school security website (www.dcsf.gov.uk/schoolsecurity).

First aid training

All LTSs will require basic first aid training to ensure that they are able to deal with minor everyday illness and injuries, and are able to recognise when to seek assistance. Staff will also need to know how to access the trained first aiders.

The true case study outlined in Activity 4 in Chapter 10, page 107, illustrates how easy it is for procedures to go wrong if they are unclear or unrehearsed. The learning points on page 107 may be helpful.

Fire procedures

Managers are often concerned that fire drill practice at lunchtime will be too disruptive. To overcome this problem they can set up a simulation at a different time of day.

Working with children who have special medical needs

This is discussed in Chapter 10, page 108 and in the DfES document *Managing Medicine in Schools and Early Years Settings.*

Playground health and safety checklist

	Yes	No
Are LTSs offered health and safety training relevant to their role of supervising the playground?	☐	☐
Are children constructively occupied in the playground and are LTSs actively encouraged in supervising and interacting with them?	☐	☐
Are there flat roofs or other dangerous structures which children climb on?	☐	☐
Are there hidden areas of the playground which are under-supervised?	☐	☐
Are regular risk assessments made of playground activities?	☐	☐
Are LTSs included in health and safety reviews and risk assessment of playground activities?	☐	☐
Are the playground rules outlining acceptable behaviour clear and on display?	☐	☐
Is there sufficient shade in the playground to protect children from the sun?	☐	☐
Is there an adequate number of working water fountains?	☐	☐
Are the playground floor surfaces and equipment inspected on a regular basis?	☐	☐
Does the playground have insecure boundaries or public access? If so, are adequate measures in place to ensure staff and children's safety?	☐	☐
Do members of staff park cars in the playground, and if so, is this managed adequately?	☐	☐
Are parents/carers regularly reminded about the school's expectations concerning playground safety?	☐	☐
Are children encouraged to understand the consequences of play behaviour and the nature of risk?	☐	☐
Are all members of the school community, including the children, encouraged to share some responsibility for health and safety?	☐	☐
Are there clear procedures for dealing with both minor and more serious accidents and emergencies in the playground?	☐	☐

Supervising the school building during lunchtime – a checklist

	Yes	No
Is behaviour in the dining room well managed?	☐	☐
Is the floor checked for food or spillages?	☐	☐
Are there clear dining room rules on display?	☐	☐
Are children clear about the rules and routines for moving around the school and dining room at lunchtime?	☐	☐
During wet play, are there sufficient numbers of LTSs to supervise the classrooms and the dining room?	☐	☐
Are risk assessments regularly made of wet play activities?	☐	☐
Are classes ever left alone during wet play, even for brief periods of time?	☐	☐

	Yes	No
Is wet play equipment checked on a regular basis?	☐	☐
Are LTSs encouraged to plan and monitor wet play activities to minimise risk?	☐	☐
Are children ever given permission to be inside the school building at lunchtime without the LTSs knowledge?	☐	☐
Are all lunchtime staff clear about fire procedures including how to evacuate the building and activate the fire alarm?	☐	☐
Is the fire drill practised during lunchtime?	☐	☐
Are there clear procedures for dealing with both minor and more serious accidents that occur in the school building during lunchtime?	☐	☐

Chapter 11 – Safeguarding children

Support staff work closely with children, and so may be the front line in detecting child abuse. They will need to receive training and support to ensure that they are able to recognise and respond to concerns appropriately.

Chapter 11 discusses what constitutes abuse and who abuses children. It briefly outlines relevant child protection law and what is likely to happen when the social services become involved. The chapter focuses in greater detail on how LTSs can recognise signs of abuse and how best they can respond to protect children. It also looks at their professional conduct and how to minimise the risk of false accusations.

Guidance for schools

Section 175 of the Education Act 2002 and Section 10 and 11 of the Children Act 2004 outline the duty on local authorities to improve the wellbeing and safeguard and promote the welfare of children. The DCSF document *Safeguarding Children and Safer Recruitment in Education* came into force in January 2007 and replaces the DfES document *Safeguarding Children in Education* (September 2004). This document provides current information and guidance for schools in England, and there is considerable emphasis on good practice in relation to recruitment selection and induction of staff. Managers may also find helpful the *Guidance for Safer Working Practice for Adults who Work with Children and Young People* (DCSF 2007) and *Staying Safe Action Plan* (DCSF 2008).

Safer recruitment

The vetting and barring scheme as outlined in the Safeguarding Vulnerable Groups Act 2006, requires that from 20 January 2009, employers submit referrals to the Independent Safeguarding Authority (ISA), information about individuals who may pose a risk of harm to children. The Vetting and Barring Scheme (VBS) will go fully live in Autumn 2010 and specific guidance and training material will be published shortly.

Training for support staff

Government guidelines state that LEAs are expected to provide child protection induction training for all new staff who work with children.

As outlined in *Safeguarding Children and Safer Recruitment in Education* (DCSF 2006), the induction programme should include written statements and training in relation to relevant policies and procedures, and clarification of expectations. Staff should be offered opportunity for ongoing discussion and support in a way that is appropriate to their role. This process should also enable line managers or mentors to recognise and address concerns.

Schools are required to give all staff that work with children a written statement about the school's policy and procedures, and the name and contact details of the 'designated person'. Schools may also decide to offer LTSs school-based safeguarding children training.

LTSs will need to know how to:

- Recognise the signs of child abuse (see Chapter 11, pages 114–16)
- Listen and respond to children's disclosures (see Chapter 11, pages 116–17)
- Respond to concerns about a child's wellbeing as outlined by the school child protection policy (see Chapter 11, pages 113–19)
- Behave professionally at work to protect themselves from accusations of abuse (see Chapter 11, pages 118–19, *Guidance for Safe Working Practice for the Protection of Children and Staff in an Educational Setting* (DCSF 2007) and *The Use of Force to Control or Restrain Pupils: Non-statutory Guidance for Schools in England* (DCSF 2007).

Confidentiality of information

Lunchtime staff often live in the school neighbourhood. They are likely to be known by local families and may have their own children in the same school. Following reporting a concern, the LTS will therefore need to be offered anonymity, Whenever possible, when alleged incidents of abuse are discussed with the family.

Information about children who have been abused will be shared on a need to know basis. As discussed in previous chapters, LTSs require adequate information to enable them to do their job (see Chapters 2 and 11, pages 12–13 and 113). LTSs will also benefit from guidance on how to respond to parents/carers who wish to discuss confidential issues.

The duty to refer

This has been discussed in detail in Chapter 11, page 113. School procedures for referral may need clarification as in some teams LTSs are expected to refer concerns of abuse to the senior LTS, whereas in others it may be the senior designated person. LTSs will need to be encouraged to report their concerns no matter how confused or uncertain they may feel.

Professional conduct and appropriate physical contact

Lunchtime staff will benefit from specialised training in restraint and discussion about appropriate physical contact with pupils. For further information, see *Guidance for Safe Working Practice for the Protection of Children and Staff in an Educational Setting* (2007) and *The Use of Force to Control or Restrain Pupils: Non-statutory Guidance for Schools in England* (DCSF 2007).

Existing practice concerning appropriate physical contact has also been discussed in Chapter 5, page 53 and in Chapter 11, pages 118–19.

Whistle blowing

As outlined in *Guidance for Safe Working Practice for the Protection of Children and Staff in an Educational Setting* (DCSF 2007), all members of staff should be aware of what to do if they have concerns about the behaviour of their colleagues.

A safeguarding children checklist

Are LTSs...	Yes	No
Offered appropriate training by the school or the education authority to enable them to recognise and respond to concerns about child abuse?	☐	☐
Familiar with the school safeguarding children policy and how it relates to their work with children?	☐	☐
Given a written statement about the school's policy and procedures and the name and contact details of the senior designated person in school?	☐	☐
Offered induction training and ongoing discussion about safeguarding children?	☐	☐
Updated on any changes in child protection procedures?	☐	☐
Clear who to refer concerns to, and how to follow procedures for recording incidents?	☐	☐
Encouraged to talk about concerns with an appropriate person when they are feeling uncertain or confused?	☐	☐
Offered appropriate feedback about child abuse concerns they reported?	☐	☐
Encouraged to listen to children in a non-judgemental and sensitive way?	☐	☐
Aware of ways to respond when talking to children about suspected abuse?	☐	☐
Clear that they cannot promise children confidentiality?	☐	☐
Offered guidance about confidentiality of information including how best to respond to parents/carers who may approach them?	☐	☐
Given guidance and opportunities to discuss appropriate physical contact with pupils?	☐	☐
Offered guidelines about professional conduct to minimise the risk of false accusations of abuse being made against them?	☐	☐
Aware of the procedures for voicing concerns about behaviour of other members of staff if necessary?	☐	☐

References and bibliography

Berger, Nan (1990) *The School Meal Service from its Beginning to the Present Day.* Tavistock: Northcote House Educational Publishers.

Blatchford, Peter (1998) *Social Life in Schools: Pupils' Experience of Breaktimes and Recess from 7–16.* London: Routledge.

British Heart Foundation (2001) *Active Playgrounds: Guide for Primary Schools.* Loughborough: BHF Publications.

Burnham, Louise and Jones, Helen (2002) *The Teaching Assistant's Handbook.* Oxford: Heinemann.

Byl, John (2003) *101 Fun Warm-Up and Cool-Down Games.* Human Kinetics website (www.humankinetics.com).

ChildLine (2004) Racism information sheet from (www.childline.org.uk/)

Children and Young People's Unit (2001) *Learning to Listen: Core Principles for the Involvement of Children and Young People.* London: CYPU.

DCSF (2007a) *The Use of Force to Control or Restrain Pupils: Non-statutory Guidance for Schools in England.* London: Department for Children, Schools and Families.

DCSF (2007b) *Guidance for Safer Working Practice for Adults who Work with Children and Young People.* London: Department for Chldren, Schools and Families.

DCSF (2007c) *Safe to Learn: Embedding Anti-bullying Work in Schools Overview.* London: Department for Children, Schools and Families.

DCSF (2008a) *Working Together: Listening to the Voices of Children and Young People.* London: Department for Children, Schools and Families.

DCSF (2008b) *Unlock the Potential of Your Support Staff.* London: Department for Children, Schools and Families.

Department of Health (2003) *What to Do if You're Worried a Child is Being Abused* (summary). London: Department of Health.

DfES (1995) Circular 10/95. London: DfES.

DfES (1998a) Circular 10/98. London: DfES.

DfES (1998b) *Guidance on First Aid for Schools: A Good Practice Guide.* Teachernet website (www.teachernet.gov.uk).

DfES (2001) *Health and Safety Responsibilities and Powers.* London: DfES.

DfES (2003) *Introductory Training for Support Staff.* London: DfES.

DfES (2004) *Safeguarding Children in Education.* Teachernet website (www.teachernet. gov.uk).

DfES (2005a) *Playtimes and Lunchtimes.* Primary National Strategy professional development pack. London: DfES.

DfES (2005b) *Managing Medicine in Schools and Early Years Settings.* Teachernet website (www.teachernet.gov.uk).

Dreikurs, Rudolf, Grunwald, Bernice and Pepper, Floy (1998) *Maintaining Sanity in the Classroom: Classroom Management Techniques*. New York: Taylor and Francis.

Elliot, Michelle (1994) *Keeping Safe: A Practical Guide to Talking to Children*. London: Coronet Books.

Golding, Rob (2000) *Playground Games: More Playground Games*. Cambridge: Pearson Publishing.

Haines, J. and Neumark-Sztainer, D. (2006) 'Prevention of obesity and eating disorders: a consideration of shared risk factors'. *Health Education Research*, 21(6), 770–82.

Jackson, Mary (2004) Quoted in David Bocking 'Time for play', *TES*, 8 October.

Kumar, Lalit (1991) *Teaching in England: Awareness of Different Cultural Traits*. Teachernet website (www.teachernet.gov.uk).

Lloyd, Richard and Ching, Charlene (2003) *School Security Concerns*. Teachernet website (www.teachernet.gov.uk).

National Centre for Playwork Education (2000) *Everyone can Play: Inclusive Play Training Pack*. Gloucestershire: National Centre for Playwork Education South West.

Northern, Stephanie (2004) 'School grounds', *TES*, 16 January.

Ofsted (2008) *How Well are they Doing? The Impact of Children's Centres and Extended Schools*. London: Ofsted.

Ormrod, J.E. (1999) *Human Learning*, 3rd edn. Upper Saddle River, NJ: Prentice-Hall.

Rogers, Bill (2003) *Behaviour Management: A Whole School Approach*. London: Paul Chapman.

Smith, Peter (2000) *Bullying – Don't Suffer in Silence: An Anti-bullying Pack for Schools*. www.dfes.gov.uk/bullying

Tauber, Robert T. (1997) *Self-fulfilling Prophecy: A Practical Guide to its Use in Education*. Portsmouth, NH: Greenwood Publishing Group.

Theory into practice database (http://tip.psychology.org/behaviourism B.F. Skinner).

Thomas Coram Research Unit (2003) *Tackling Bullying: Listening to the Views of Children and Young People*. London: DfES.

Thomson, Sarah (2003) 'A well equipped hamster cage: the rationalisation of primary school playtime', *Education 3–13*, June.

Thomson, Sarah (2005) 'Territorialising the primary school playground: deconstructing the geography of playtime', *Children's Geographies*, 3 (1), 63–78, April.

Titman, Wendy (1992) *Play, Playtimes and Playgrounds*. Crediton: Southgate Publishers.

White, Angela and Wilkinson, Jane (2000) *Playtimes and Playgrounds*. Bristol: Lucky Duck.

Youth Sport Trust (2004) *Primary Playground Development Pack*. Loughborough: Youth Sport Trust.

Websites and useful contacts

Anti-Bullying Alliance
www.nch.org/aba
020 7843 6000

Anti-Bullying Campaign
020 7378 1446

Association of Play Industries provide a full list
www.playindustries.org
02476 414999

Bullying Online
www.bullying.co.uk

Children's Play Council – children's play information service and the council for disabled children
www.ncb.org.uk
020 7843 6000

Collins, Wendy (1998) *Active Playtimes* (www.southgatepublishers.co.uk).

Department for Culture, Media and Sport, *Zoneparcs Funding*
www.culture.gov.uk

Directory for Social Change
See Fundraising for Schools
www.dsc.org.uk

Games Kids Play
www.gameskidsplay.net

Growing Schools
www.teachernet.gov.uk

Kidscape
www.kidscape.org.uk
020 7730 3300

Learning through Landscapes
www.ltl.org.uk

Lottery Fund
www.community-fund.org.uk

Playground Pals
www.pioneer.cwc.net/playgroundpals.htm

Playwork training qualifications
www.playwork.org.uk
020 7632 2000

Rose, Shirley
www.shirleyrose.co.uk
shirley@crorose.eclipse.co.uk

Sabin, Val (2004) *Positive Play: An Activities Manual and Guide for Positive Play at Breaktime*
www.valsabinpublications.com
01604 580947

Index